Opulence Infusion

A New Faith Currency

Jennifer Ruth Russell

Published in United States of America by Remba Publishing

ISBN-13: 978-1-7322732-3-8

Opulence Infusion – a new faith currency

Copyright © 2023 by Jennifer Ruth Russell

Cover painting *"Opulence"* by Michelle Walker © 2023 Michelle Walker

Graphic Design by Elizabeth MacFarland

All rights reserved. No part of this publication may be reproduced or transmitted by any means, electronic, photocopying or otherwise, without prior written permission of the author.

Disclaimer

The information in this book, and all information written or channeled by Jennifer Ruth Russell in any manner or form, is not intended or implied to be a substitute for professional health or medical advice, diagnosis or treatment, or for professional financial advice. Health, financial, and life results vary with each individual and no results are guaranteed. No writing from Jennifer Ruth Russell is meant or intended to diagnose, treat, cure or prevent any disease or other life condition.

Contents

Foreword 1
About This Book 3
How to Use this Book 6

Part One A New Faith Currency 8

1 Calibration 9
2 Your Faith 14
3 Golden Mist 16
4 You Are the Container 19
5 Opening the Third Eye 21
6 The Opulence Light Codes 24
7 Sacred Geometry 28
8 POGO 31
9 Fire Dragons 34
10 JOY 37
11 Daily Forgiveness 39
12 Your Power Team 41
13 Rest in the Bounty 44
14 Drop of Gold 46

15	The Circle	49
16	God of Gold	53
17	Crystals	56
18	Go Beyond	59
19	Be strong	61
20	Declare	64
21	Where we're going	68

Part Two Let's Get Practical 71

22	Sacred Fire	72
23	Walk with Us	75
24	Financial Healing	77
25	Your Body Elemental	80
26	Quiet Intimacy	83
27	Your Physical Body	85
28	Our Partnership	87
29	Seeing with Archangel Raphael	89
30	Uncertainty	91
31	Release the Burden	93
32	Ask for More	96
33	Stay Alert	99

Part Three   The Golden White Unicorns 102

34   The Golden White Unicorns 103
35   Worry or Opulence 105
36   Unicorn Blessings 108
37   Money Cleansing 111
38   Protect your Money 114
39   Ignite Your Circulation 116
40   Activate Your Bills 120
41   Storehouses of Gold 123
42   Numbers and Dollars 126
43   You are the Bridge 129
44   I AM a Living Transmission of Opulence 133
45   Commanding Presence 135
46   Multiply 138
47   The Flame of Adoration 141
48   Riding the Waves 144
49   Heal Your Inner Critic 147
50   Choose Again and Again 150
51   Your Sweet Spot 153
52   Circle of Cleansing Light 155
53   Faith Expansion 158
54   Pure Heart 161
55   Command the Age of Miracles 163
Dedication 165

Acknowledgements 166
About the Author..168

Foreword

When there is an adamant call to the Beloved Divine there is always an answer.

Jennifer has specifically asked on behalf of all lightworkers for an Opulence Infusion - a new faith currency.

It's a spiritual technology that can be used in this transitional time within the existing systems of exchange.

It's something simple to help relieve the stress and striving of "making a living." It's assistance to set free the divine energy healers could use to complete their divine mission.

An entire team has been working on her insistent request and we are grateful that she is ready.

You are ready, Beloved, to receive this new frequency of Opulence.

You are the container to bring it in. The currency of heaven is you. All that is required is you and your faith.

This new system will come in many different forms that will be applicable and practical.

The new faith currency will be relevant to your life. It will show up in ways that will be very meaningful to you.

It will move you quickly into manifestation beyond what you know right now.

Ascension in a human body has never happened before on Earth.

We want to help you in the transition to a 5th dimensional life and above. We want to help you create a divine new earth. We want to offer light codes, transmissions, techniques, skills, and spiritual technologies.

You have trained for many lifetimes to assist in this Grand Event.

We are delighted to see you lift into your sovereignty and create on a higher level.

I love and adore you,

Mother Mary and the Pure Gold Project Team

About This Book

As a spiritual mentor and musician and ... a missionary kid, I've had a long journey in the contrast of lack and abundance. I've had the opportunity to make lots of money that left me fatigued and empty. I've experimented in the bliss of ignorance, luck, and wishful thinking around money.

But everything changed one rainy afternoon in the Ukraine at a funky art gallery off the main highway. Mother Mary called my name.

As she began mentoring me, I started to heal deep within the memories of my heart. My money angst started to give way to peace and freedom. In my sessions and my Angels of Abundance Ascension Academy, people began to be healed, of illness, broken hearts, and financial pain.

Mother Mary and I have written several books, *21 Days to Abundance through the Immaculate Heart of Mother Mary, How to Create with Mother Mary and Friends, and Empowered Prayer.* All of them have focused around how to flow in your true wealth and abundance as a cocreator with the Beloved Divine.

But when I realized that the entire system is broken and infiltrated with the darkness of greed and power, I started to ask for a completely new way of exchange.

When Mother Mary, Archangel Raphael, and Saint Germain started leading me into a new faith currency that is beyond this world, but can be used practically in the old systems, I got excited.

This book began in the quiet of my altar in 2019 and now it's time to bring it to you.

Withdrawing from the old burden of debt and depravity and stepping into an Opulence Infusion, a new faith currency, has lifted me into a blissful experience of all needs met, all the time, every time.

If you've tried many prosperity programs and they haven't worked for you ... I believe the reason is that we've been working on a loop within the old system itself. Trying to chug up the mountain with our own efforts of healing has helped but it hasn't brought much change into daily living. Why? Because the entire system is obsolete.

I also believe our true relationship with our partners in the higher octaves can no longer be denied. We were made to walk and create with the Angels, the Ascended Ones, the Elementals, and the Cosmic Beings of Light.

I'm thrilled that this is mine to do. I feel privileged to bring the amazing Opulence Infusion – a new faith currency, to all of us.

I'm grateful for my long journey into the transmissions that Saint Germain has provided for us. No longer do we have to wonder and seek the secrecy of the ancient Mystery Schools that were hidden from us.

I honor the teachings of the Masters of Wisdom channeled through Mr. and Mrs. Guy Ballard and Geraldine Innocenti, El Morya's twin flame, between the years 1938 and 1970. These teachings from the Bridge to Freedom dispensation are part of who I am.

The work of Diana Cooper has opened the relationships with the Dragons and Unicorns for me and my community. The Golden Dragons and the Golden White Unicorns are included in this book, *Opulence Infusion*. Also, *The Archangel Guide to Ascension – 55 Steps to the Light* by Diana Cooper and Tim Whild has opened our Ascension journey with current information.

This is what Saint Germain has to say. *"The Golden Unicorns will lift this project, Opulence Infusion, into an entirely new level of manifestation. The Unicorns will make it real. They will bring their magic and transformation in real tangible ways that will open every Lightworker to receive more."*

How to Use this Book

Come into these pages with intense commitment and expectancy.

Opulence Infusion is not a casual read. This project asks for your full participation and focus.

This book is given to you in the order that I received it.

I recommend that you give yourself time to integrate each chapter, one at a time.

Opulence Infusion – a New Faith Currency comes in three parts.

Part One – New Faith Currency

The steps within this section will open your partnership to the Pure Gold Project team. The Lab is in the Pure Gold Temple in the 10th Sphere (dimension) of Golden Light.

You'll become familiar with the Lab. It is where you'll come daily to calibrate and re-calibrate to the frequency of Opulence, be given the new spiritual technology, and establish the scaffolding of the new faith currency within you.

Use the music from my *Opulence Light Songs* collection to receive this calibration and help you to establish your container. You can find *Opulence Light Songs* on any digital music platform or my bandcamp site.

https://jenniferruthrussell.bandcamp.com/music/

Part Two – Let's Get Practical

When we combine your conscious awareness with the assistance of our powerful Galactic Team of Pure Gold, we become a powerful force field of constructive change.

Phase Two of the Pure Gold Project will bring this technology into practical use. Not only in your life, but in service to the world.

It will show up in ways that will blow your mind.

Part Three – The Golden White Unicorns

Because you are part of the Opulence Infusion, the new faith currency, that is being manifest on Earth right now, your Unicorn is also here as a part of this powerful collective.

My personal Unicorn, Thom, asked Mother Mary and me to give him the opportunity to speak. As you remember your own personal Unicorn, you'll experience the strength of your partnership with the Golden White Unicorns Collective.

These Mighty and Pure Angelic Beings are here to assist us to Ascend in Opulence and Beauty.

Once you've completed the book in order, we invite you to let your team guide you to different chapters to keep you ignited on your path in establishing the new faith currency in your life and in all of your projects.

Part One

A New Faith Currency

1

Calibration

Welcome Beloved, you have stepped into a vortex of Opulence.

We can hear the many questions you have about the new faith currency. What is it? How can I use it? How can it change my life?

All your questions will be answered. It is your insistence that will create this experience for you.

As Beloved Saint Germain has said, it will take your intense expectation, your willingness, and your faith.

There is much to share with you. This will not be a knowledge-based curriculum, but an experiential journey.

Faith currency is based on faith and not on works.

It's a 6th and 7th dimensional spiritual technology.

It's made of Light and the essence of Pure Gold. It is not a 3rd dimensional substance but can be used in the upper 4th and 5th dimensions.

Once you rise into the 6th dimension a means of exchange will not be necessary.

It is a currency of all needs met, all the time – no matter what. It was given to Jennifer as POGO (more to come about this).

Today we want to take you to the Temple of Pure Gold Lab and introduce you to the Pure Gold Project team.

You'll be building your container for the new faith currency within the momentum of the Pure Gold Project Lab.

This beautiful Temple of Pure Gold is a pyramid. You'll be coming here daily to calibrate and recalibrate your vibration frequency to the essence of Pure Gold. This frequency is the Divine Substance that Faith Currency is made of.

So, let's begin.

Make sure you're in your sacred space, a safe quiet place where you do your spiritual practice.

Close your eyes and breathe into your sacred heart Oneness of your Beloved I AM Presence. Feel this Oneness expand to include All There Is.

Ground and anchor into Mother Earth.

Ask Archangel Michael to intensify your protective tube of pure light around you and charge it with His invincible protection, all powerful and impenetrable.

Graft your heart to mine, Beloved, and feel our sacred union.

Surrender now and let me lift you up from the 3rd dimension into the 10th dimension. It helps to count slowly from 3 to 10. Make sure you allow your breath to be slow and steady.

We are in the 10th Sphere of Pure Gold. This is the aspect of the Beloved Divine that is Infinite Abundance, Eternal Peace, and the God supply of all that is Good.

We've entered a City of Gold. A beautiful Golden Mist immediately lifts you up in its buoyant energy.

See the Angels of Abundance everywhere greeting you as we begin to walk through the beauty of this City. Let your imagination go and see it, Beloved.

We have arrived at a golden pyramid, the Temple of Pure Gold.

You are greeted by your own Galactic Family, your Beloved I AM Presence, your Guardian Angel, your Body Elemental, all the Ascended Masters that you work with, your guides, and Angels.

The sound of the Angels of Abundance singing fills the atmosphere with harmonies and tones that embrace you and open your heart.

As you gaze around, look up at the apex of the pyramid, there's a huge crystal of rainbow Christ Light flooding the Light of the Rays everywhere. See the full spectrum of color dancing on your skin.

You see a balcony circling the entire pyramid and you realize that it is full of Magnificent Beings of Light that are here to greet you and help you calibrate to the high frequency of the new faith currency. They have been gathering here regularly for years to help Jennifer with this project.

Come and have a seat, Beloved. We've prepared a special calibration chair for you. Feel this chair gently cradling you and helping you open your 12 - 5th dimensional chakras.

As you continue to breathe deeply and fully, I will speak the names of this Magnificent Pure Gold Project team. You are welcome to add anyone from your personal heavenly team to this collective.

Let these names wash over you as a beautiful shower of Light.

Mighty I AM Presence

The Great Central Sun and the Great Central Sun Magnet

Alpha and Omega

Helios and Vesta

Universal Divine Mother – Sophia

Lady Venus, Sanat Kumara, Lady Venussa

Angels of Abundance

God of Gold

Lords of Gold

Angels of Gold

Fortuna - Goddess of Supply

My Divine Complement -Archangel Raphael

Archangel Michael and Lady Faith

Saint Germain and Lady Portia

Kwan Yin

Master Hilarion,

Jeshua (Lord Sanada)

Lady Nada

Angels of Miracle Manifestation

Angels of Precipitation

Masters of Precipitation

The Mighty Elohim

The Mighty Archangels

Lady Liberty

Mighty Victory

Archangel Gabriel and Lady Hope

Lord Lanto and the Brotherhood of Precipitation from the Royal Teton Retreat

Deva of Pure Gold -MATIPA

Amaryllis - the Goddess of Spring

Beloved Metatron and Archangel Sandalphon

Deva Liberty of the American Golden Eagle

Adama, the High Priest of Telos

Manna - teenage technician from Telos

Dolphin Queen Regina and the Dolphins from Sirius, the Sophia Dragons, the Dragons of Alpha and Omega, your personal Dragon and your team of Dragons

The Golden White Unicorns, your personal Unicorn

Your Beloved Divine Complement

Your High Future Self from the 6th dimension.

Let us calibrate you now, Beloved. Be still and receive the essence of Pure Gold, the new faith currency through Jennifer's Light Song, *Calibration Chamber.* *

Breathe it in all 12 of your Chakras.

I love and adore you,

Mother Mary and the Angels of Abundance

*"Calibration Chamber" is on Jennifer's EP **Opulence**.

2

Your Faith

Beloved, your faith is the motor that runs this currency.

Before, you start questioning your own faith, stop and give it over to your Beloved I AM Presence. Just surrender your thoughts of your own faith to your Beloved. Release your opinion about it.

Faith continually asks you to step up to another level of trust. Trust is the action of faith in your life.

Whatever faith that you have right now is enough. I want you to hear this above all else.

Your faith is the currency of heaven. It allows you to walk in the unknown and be completely cared for every moment, no matter what is happening around you.

Your financial system is working on an old paradigm that is obsolete and archaic. It will be dismantled while you are still a part of it. It is already happening.

Do not be afraid. We are with you every step of the way. Your agreement to be a part of this transition and to be human is a divine call. You were made to transcend the old and anchor the new. There is a strong current of fear that the mass of humanity experiences every day. To go beyond the old will require all your faith to stay in the new faith currency and out of fear.

This fear doesn't belong to you. You will have many opportunities to choose faith instead of fear. This is how you get stronger and stronger in your faith muscle.

Remember you can't be in a state of worry and faith at the same time.

You are on the front line of this shift, Beloved, and we are asking you to deconstruct the old system of money beliefs within yourself.

Changing the coal of your old fears and beliefs into diamonds of faith is spiritual alchemy.

Your Beloved I AM Presence is just waiting to take you to the next level of faith. Give the heavy lifting to your Beloved.

Every time you feel fear, worry, or anxiety around money, notice what is going on. Dismantle it by giving it a moment of your attention, choose differently, and then serve it up to your Beloved in release, commanding that it be transmuted into Pure Gold, your new faith currency.

Anytime you need a boost of faith, call on Archangel Michael and Lady Faith and ask them to infuse you with their faith. Remember, Archangel Michael is the defender of your faith and Lady Faith is the Spirit within your faith.

Put your attention on where you are going instead of trying to wrestle the old paradigm to the ground.

I love and adore you,

Mother Mary and the Angels of Abundance

3

Golden Mist

I am deeply grateful to be a part of the Pure Gold Project. I AM Lady Venus, the guardian of planet Venus with my Divine Complement, Sanat Kumara. I am also known as the Goddess of Love and Beauty. Our beloved planet is your big sister planet, and we have much to share with you about Pure Gold.

You have stepped into the Age of Aquarius with Beloved Saint Germain as your guiding Light. It is a Golden Age of Miracles. Every Golden Age has been backed by Pure Gold.

Pure Gold comes right from the heart of Source, also known as the Great Central Sun, the home of Alpha and Omega.

Pure Gold isn't defined by any currency system and never will be. It simply is.

Remember this truth as the world currencies change and move out of the old money systems.

There are stations throughout this Solar System where the essence of Pure Gold is held in concentrated form, so that we can help distribute it when and where it is needed.

The Pure Gold Lab is located at The City of Gold in the 10th Sphere. Both The City of Gold and the Planet Venus are among the many different stations of Pure Gold throughout the Universe.

That's why we ask you to come to the Lab daily and allow us to help you calibrate and recalibrate to the Opulence of the Universe.

We have planted the essence of Pure Gold into the Light Songs that you can listen to on Jennifer's music platforms. *

You are becoming an anchor for this essence on the ground. Remember you are a Godling.

The deposits of gold that are found on Earth were deposited by Cosmic Beings of Light passing through.

Come into my heart, Beloved, and feel the Love and Beauty of my embrace.

Let us go together into the 10th Sphere and into the Pyramid Temple of Pure Gold.

Let me show you around.

Breathe in this Golden Mist. It is the Glory of the Goddess. It is the Glory of the Great Central Sun. The Golden Mist is pure. It is brilliance. It is unique within Itself.

This Pure Gold is Divine. It is Purity. It is Love. Receive it now. Take some time to continue to breathe it in.

Love your desire to precipitate Pure Gold in your life. It's a high resolve. It will change the paradigm of lack for you and all Lightworkers that are ready for this level of commitment.

Pour your love into Me and I will flow it back to you.

Let's grow this Love and Beauty and Pure Gold right now. Let me help you to magnify it and to multiply the Glory of the Great Central Sun.

See this Golden Mist flowing through the atmosphere of Earth. It is already here. Open your eyes to see.

As a conductor of divine energy, you can direct this Golden Mist. Bring it into the earthy parts of your life. Infuse your drinking water with it. Sprinkle it on the food that you eat. See it filling your home and your garden. Send it throughout your neighborhood to bless everyone.

It is Done! It is Done! It is Done!

Speak this decree often, *I AM Pure Gold and I command it to move through my hands and use now.*

I hold you in my heart,

Lady Venus

*Jennifer's EP "Opulence" is a collection of Light Songs that will help you calibrate and receive an infusion of Opulence. Find them here, https://jenniferruthrussell.bandcamp.com/ and on any music platform i.e., Apple Music or Spotify.

4

You Are the Container

I AM Metatron the creator of all Light in this Universe. I work closely with Helios, the Father of this Solar System, to bring the forms, the sacred geometry, that holds the original blueprint of all Creator Light into matter.

You are intimately connected to me. I created the very electrons that are Pure Light Substance within every atom, within every cell of your being.

You are the container that holds the new faith currency. You are the form, the body, the perfect symmetry of the Beloved Divine. This is not something you need to get or connect with outside of yourself.

Hear me my friend, you already ARE the complete system. You are the container that is bringing the essence of Pure Gold into your life and anchoring it on the Earth in a new way.

You are the Monad, the Presence I AM, this is a fixed design that you came with.

Your understanding of the sacred structure that you are is the very scaffolding that is bringing in and holding the new faith currency. In its most simple formulation, it is 12 x12 = 144.

YOU ARE A VAST, MAGNIFICENT BEING. When you made the choice to incarnate on planet Earth, you became a Monad. It is also called the Soul or the I AM Presence. Some people call it their Soul Family. You are twelve souls, and each soul has twelve extensions. These aspects of you are in many different dimensions and timelines.

Don't try to understand this with your human mind. It is a spiritual knowing. As you ascend, you'll continue to be given deeper insights about your Monad. For those of you that are mathematicians and enjoy numbers you can see the beauty of its geometry.

I am helping you ascend by assisting you in opening your 12 Strands of DNA and your 12 - 5th Dimensional Chakras. I know your Monad intimately.

Use this ancient decree to help you line up with your Magnificent Self. As you use it, you'll begin to feel who you really are.

Speak it out loud 3 times before you begin your day.

I AM the Monad. I AM Light Divine. I AM Love. I AM Wisdom. I AM Will. I AM Fixed Design. *

I Am with you always,

Archangel Metatron from the 12th Dimension

*This decree was brought to us by Ascended Master Djwhal Khul through Alice Bailey. It is the mantra of the Galactic Council of Light.

5

Opening the Third Eye

Come up to the Pure Gold Project Pyramid and let us recalibrate you to this frequency that we call the new faith currency.

Now you are ready for today's lesson.

Beloved, flow through my heart and together we flow into Archangel Raphael's specialty of new spiritual technology and your third eye.

Call on Beloved Raphael. Simply say His name and He'll come.

I AM Archangel Raphael. I AM the Archangel of consecration and concentration. I AM also overseeing the Abundance consciousness of all humanity. I AM also the guardian of your third eye chakra.

I am connected to Jupiter.

You create with your third eye. As you activate it and use it as a 5th dimensional chakra, you'll begin to manifest quickly. I want to show you how to do this and how to let me assist you.

Let's begin with your desired thought form. What would you like this new faith currency to do for you and humanity?

Give all your focus and attention on that question for the next 5 to 10 minutes.

Ground yourself into Mother Earth.

Let's open your third eye. Take your finger and rub gently in a circular motion between your eyebrows until you find a soft opening. Release your hand and sit up straight with your feet anchored on the floor.

Beloved Archangel Michael, surround us in your Divine protection. Thank you.

Focus on your third eye. See it moving as a circular tunnel of emerald green light in a counterclockwise motion to cleanse it. Now change direction and move it in a clockwise direction.

The color and shape are now changing to a crystal-clear ball which acts like a lens of a camera.

Place your thought form on this lens and concentrate on what you are creating.

The crystal ball thought form now begins to turn slowly to the right in a circular motion up the tunnel of your third eye.

I AM right here assisting you. My Emerald Green Dragons surround you and help to expand and multiply your efforts. *

Now flow the thought form through this tunnel all the way to planet Jupiter, the planet of good fortune.

Use your inner sight and your imagination to plant your thought form here.

Call on our assistance. Say: *Beloved Raphael and the Emerald Green Dragons, assist me in anchoring and holding my thought form for the new faith currency in focus and alignment with my Higher Self and the good of all humanity.*

As you come back to where you began this journey, notice the permanent pathway you have created and anchored today. Beginning from your heart's desire, you created a tunnel of light from your third eye all the way to Jupiter and back.

This currency will be received through the light waves and through your faith.

Give thanks to the Emerald Green Dragons. You are welcome to ask one of them to stay with you and protect your thought form as it is growing and gains strength.

Always at your service,

Archangel Raphael

The Archangel Guide to Ascension, Diana Cooper and Tim Whild

6

The Opulence Light Codes

Beloved, we are eager to download the Opulence Light Codes to you. The new faith currency is composed of Light and Sound.

Prepare yourself to receive this gift. Have your journal with you.

Your job is to let go of the old clutter of scarcity in your mind and in your environment and to stay in miracle readiness.

Beloved, this cosmic event that we are in the middle of is asking for your full participation. It is similar to when the Israelites followed Moses out of the slavery of Egypt into the Promised Land.

They had to leave behind everything that they knew and trust the Beloved Divine to take care of literally everything.

The transformation from slavery and hard labor, into being fed directly from the hand of Source, is very similar to what you are being asked to do with your money life right now.

It is in the unknown, a place of uncertainty and yet Spirit will continue to provide everything that you need.

This exercise will help you let go of the old clutter of scarcity.

Connect with your Beloved I AM Presence and ground yourself into your Earth Star and Mother Earth.

Call on our Beloved friends Archangel Michael, the Blue Flame Angels, the Earth, and Fire Dragons to place a wall of Divine Protection around you. Ask them to cleanse your four lower bodies, the atmosphere around you, and the ley lines within the Earth beneath you.

Stand in your Divine Authority. You are the I AM, that I AM.

Breathe deeply and remain in a listening state.

Check your heart. Is there any fear of the future or fear that the money will run out, that is still holding on?

Archangel Michael and I will help you. Give it to me now. With your mind's eye take your dominant hand, reach into your heart, and gently dislodge this fear and give it to me. If it is more than a handful, keep going — pull it out and give it to me. I will heal it. If it returns at any time - give it to me. Ask Archangel Michael to help you dissolve and transmute this old fear into complete faith.

Breathe deeply and remain in a listening state

Open your inner eye of abundance and see where you are holding on to clutter in your physical environment. What are you keeping that you don't need? Have you allowed things to clutter up around you? Write down what you are holding on to in your journal. This list is distracting you. Plan now to give it away or throw it out with a blessing. This will clear your mind and free you up to receive.

Are you hoarding anything? Beloved, this is a false protection mechanism. It's a barrier. It's blocking your flow of abundance. Look at it. Give it to me. Let's call in the Angels of Abundance to help you take down this barrier.

Breathe deeply and remain in a listening state

Look at your relationships. Where is there discord? Is there something that you've been avoiding? Be honest with yourself and write it all down. Forgive yourself and everyone else. Ask Archangel Zadkiel and Holy Amethyst to flood the Violet Flame through all your relationships. Surrender them to your Beloved I AM Presence and ask me to help heal them.

Breathe deeply and remain in a listening state.

Ask the question. Is there anything else that is cluttering up my receiving channel? Write it down and release it.

Decide with me today to do your best to stay in uninterrupted harmony. Your decision makes it so.

Miracle readiness is a state of joy and trust. It takes complete focus on your Beloved I AM Presence. Your Beloved is the channel of your supply. To allow for this provision, surrender everything to your Beloved I AM Presence repeatedly.

I urge you to stay in a place of harmony and miracle readiness to keep the door of Opulence open.

"I AM the active miracle Presence governing all manifestation in my life and world perfectly."

As you prepare for sleep visit the Pure Gold Project Lab and ask Me to download the Opulence Light Codes of the new faith currency. This transmission will come through my Immaculate Heart into the very cells, atoms, and electrons of your subtle bodies. *

Jennifer experienced this activation in the state between sleep and waking. Scrolls and scrolls of Golden Light filled with sacred geometry flooded through her entire being.

These Opulence Light Codes are yours, Beloved. Forever. They are embedded in the light song, "Opulence Light Codes", by Jennifer.

I love and adore you,

Mother Mary and the Angels of Abundance

*Your four lower bodies, referred to as your subtle bodies, are your physical, mental, emotional, and etheric (also known as spiritual) bodies.

7

Sacred Geometry

Beloveds, I Am Metatron.

I want to tell you more about 12 x 12 = 144. This sacred sequence is ready to be opened in fullness now.

This is a power equation.

As you open to experiencing the flow of all needs met, it becomes a symbol of that Truth. It sets the new faith currency into an eternal fixture and structure within every cell, atom, and electron, of your auric field. Think of it as a scaffolding that gives you strength and meaning as you move into this new paradigm.

Sacred Geometry holds the Light in form.

I AM the Archangel of the 12th sphere and I oversoul your 12th Chakra, your Stellar Gateway.* I am the 12 and as you ascend, each of your chakras becomes fully activated in the dimension that you are entering. For most people on the Earth that is the 5th dimension.

The 12 x 12 gives you strength and substance to stand on and operate from.

Feel into the vertical aspects of your 12 chakras. Allow me to flood you with my Golden Orange Light Ray. Breath it down from your Beloved Presence's portal, your Stellar Gateway chakra and let it saturate into your Soul Star chakra, move down through your Soul Star chakra and now through your Crown chakra, your Third Eye chakra, your Throat chakra, and into your Heart chakra.

Pause here and fully feel my Radiance and Presence.

As you breathe in my full presence into your Heart, allow it to flow through your Solar Plexus chakra, Your Navel chakra, Your Sacral chakra, and your Root chakra. Now see it flooding a foot beneath your feet into your Earth Star chakra.

See your Earth Star chakra open as a disc beneath your feet, pooling the Golden Orange Magnificence and securing into Gaia. Anchor into the full strength of your sovereignty here on Earth.

Now envision each of your chakras starting to move in a circle of twelve symmetrical sections around you. See this Golden Orange Light moving you upward establishing each chakra as scaffolding to hold your new faith currency.

Now speak this Truth out loud.

I am the perfect symmetry of 12 x 12. I am complete. All 144 aspects of my being are here, secured in one place now. I AM fully functioning as the sovereign creator blueprint, I AM.

I AM the Currency of Light.

I AM the Currency of Love.

I AM the Currency of Pure Gold. I AM, that I AM!

Today, be fully awake in this scaffolding. Walk in it, breathe in it, allow it to become real to you.

I AM with you always,

I AM Metatron

*The 12 Ascended Chakra teaching is from *The Archangel Guide to Ascension*, by Diana Cooper and Tim Whild.

8

POGO

I met Jennifer on the Fall Equinox 2020. I responded to her call to help bring in a new faith currency.

I am Manna, a teenager from Telos. I'm 113 years old and will be an adult when I turn 200. I love breaking barriers and building new innovative solutions.

Telos is a Lemurian community that is in the 7th Dimension inside Mount Shasta, California.

We have been helping you in the invisible for centuries. Adama, our High Priest and the Council of Twelve have mentored the Ascended Masters.

We are excited that you are now ready to connect with us easily. We have so much to show you.

My name speaks of an ancient story. Manna was given to the Israelites when they fled the slavery of Egypt. They came into the barren desert. Manna was provided for them every day. It nourished them. It could not be stored, hoarded, or traded.

40 years in the desert helped them to let go of the consciousness of oppression, scarcity, and lack, like what you are doing now with the old money system. Don't worry it won't take you that long. You are moving quickly now.

I am a teenager of the most idealist nature. I invite you to talk to me and my friends. We'll give you new ideas of how to think about this new faith currency and how to use it.

It's like droplets in the air and you are an airbender.

Let go of methodology, processes, and steps. This is GRACE. This beautiful essence of PURE GOLD is a gift.

I want to show you today how to use POGO.

Meet me at the Rainbow Lake of Telos. It's a beautiful lake that is always active with all the Sacred Light Rays of the Universe.

Let me give you an imaginary pogo stick. Go ahead and get on it and practice bouncing. I'm bouncing with you.

Notice that every time you pound on the ground you are activating different colors of the rainbow. Now focus on Pure Gold essence, the Golden Mist. See it spark and grow wherever you land.

Use it for everything. What do you need?

POGO it.

Activate the faith currency with your intention and command. Just say "I POGO this and this and this."

You are activating the Golden Mist, the Divine Energy, to expand at that point, that place, in that situation.

Use it everywhere and give thanks.

POGO, all needs met. Every time. All the time.

I can help you increase the power of this simple spiritual technology. Just call on me and I'll be right there with you on my pogo stick. It'll be fun.

Your new friend,

Manna from Telos

9

Fire Dragons

"Dragons are beautiful, wise, open-hearted etheric beings of the angelic realms who are sent here by Source to assist us." Diana Cooper (*Dragons Your Celestial Guardians*)

Beloved, today I want to invite you to use your fire dragons, which are one of the most powerful tools in your toolbox.

The dragon brigade has come back to Earth in full force to assist humanity and the elemental kingdom. Although you may not see them yet, they are a powerful source of help for you.

Their purpose is to help Mother Father and the entire Company of Heaven (including you) to fulfill the divine plan, our ascension, and to co-create the Divine New Earth.

Dragons are loving, beautiful, and wise. They were made to serve you. They are of the angelic realm and don't have free will.

As a free will being, you are the chooser. You always need to invite them and ask them to help you.

You have a personal dragon and a dragon for each of the elements. You can also activate them as a group. Just call on them.

The 4th dimensional dragons can move, balance, and clear out energy in your dimension more effectively than the higher orders of the angelic kingdom.

Beloved, as you are calibrating to the new faith currency and releasing the old ways of exchange, ground and protect this Pure Gold Project as it makes its way into the world and through your life, just as you would an infant beginning to crawl.

The 4th dimensional fire dragons are perfect to help you clear out the old and protect the new. They are a fiery orange and they breathe fire. It's a sacred fire that consumes lower energies and protects.

You can instruct them to use the Violet Flame, the cosmic eraser, to expand the transmuting power within your empowered prayers and decrees.

They also work closely with Archangel Michael (the Blue Flame of Protection, Faith, and Provision) and his Blue Flame Angels.

Call on the fire dragons to place an etheric wall of divine protection around you anytime. It would be helpful for you to ask them to continually protect you as you calibrate and build strength in the new faith currency.

Call on them to blaze and cleanse all your current money activities so that every exchange carries only the essence of Pure Gold. They help release all the old greed, power over others, manipulation, fear, scarcity, and lack within the old system.

When you are feeling stuck in fear, ask for their help and instruct them to go to the beginning of where that fear began and cleanse your etheric records. Visualize them blazing their sacred fire as they complete the job.

They can also help you in your sleep time physically release old karmic debts and patterns that are blocking you from receiving the abundance that is always yours. Remember Beloved, it's your divine inheritance.

Send the fire dragons out in front of you to make a clear path for you.

Wherever you send them, they leave a trail of JOY and playfulness.

Take some time today to meet your personal fire dragon and the team it works with. Ask your fire dragon how it can help you.

I love and adore you,

Mother Mary and the Angels of Abundance

10

JOY

We are grateful to answer the question, "While I'm waiting for the new faith currency to come in, what should I do? Is there any action I can take? Shall I buy a lotto ticket?"

This question is where you've been, Beloved, it's not where you're going. It gives us an opportunity to speak directly into the difference.

Receiving a new faith currency that is backed by the essence of Pure Gold feels magical and other worldly. It is very real. It is a practice in the vibration and frequency of receptivity. You are to anchor it in your day-to-day life.

Feel the energy of buying a lotto ticket on the chance that you'd win millions of dollars. Is it in the vibration of abundance? Does it feel like luck is the leading force or are you?

The belief that, "If only I had this, everything would be all right." is the old falling away.

"If I scrimp on this and really stick to a budget, I'll be ok." Can you feel how this is in the vibration of lack?

We're not saying don't use your wisdom and discernment in your money affairs. Life is full of unexpected turns and twists. It's not designed to follow a budget. We have seen many lightworkers try to squeeze their life into a budget. That takes a lot more effort than it does to stay in a state of trust and joy.

The new faith currency is calling you into a life of mastery. You came, Beloved, to transcend the ancient belief in lack and depravity. Remember it is an illusion.

Let every action that you take come from your heart and a feeling of joy. Ask: Does this give me life? Does it increase my joy? Is it in the frequency of the new faith currency?

As you ascend you will be called into more and more service. You will be nourished, safe, and cared for every day.

Living in the mastery of plenty is simple and joyful. It is the beauty and efficiency of Opulence. This is the new faith currency.

Let the Angels of Abundance amplify your voice as you speak this affirmation often.

I stay in a state of total trust. The Universe responds and starts providing immediately. *

I love and adore you,

Mother Mary and the Angels of Abundance

*Inspired by Aurelia Louise Jones, *Seven Sacred Flames*

11

Daily Forgiveness

I AM Saint Germain, the God of Freedom, the Director of the Age of Aquarius, the Master of the Violet Flame, and your gentle leader and humble servant on your path of Ascension.

After spending many lifetimes on Earth bringing the call of Freedom and Justice, with my Beloved Lady Portia, we continue with full focus to assist every person into their spiritual freedom from the higher dimensions.

I want to pause and let you know how grateful we are for your presence on the ground during this cosmic event. You answered the call many lifetimes ago to be here at this time. Without you the ascension of mankind into the 5th Dimension couldn't happen.

You are in a lifetime of mastery.

Your insistence, your calibrations, your calls, your decrees, your intentions, and your prayers are what pull in the Sacred Fire Love, the Sacred Flames, the new ideas, the new spiritual technologies, and the momentum of Pure Gold Light which allows the new faith currency to take hold in your life and in the world.

This Pure Gold Project, that you are now a part of, is a combination of dismantling and cleansing the old system within yourself and opening to receive the new. Everything that you are doing for yourself you are doing for everyone. It works that way.

The quickest way to dismantle and cleanse the old is through forgiveness.

Beloved, begin a practice of daily forgiveness with the Cosmic Diamond Violet Flame.

Archangel Zadkiel and I have joined with Archangel Gabriel in bringing together the Diamond Light and the Violet Flame. The Diamond Light cuts away all negativity and the Violet Flame transmutes it, permanently dissolving it back into pure Light.

Remember we are part of you. We are you in the future. We are entirely focused on helping you step into your financial freedom as soon as possible.

This decree is our gift for you to use as much as you can. We suggest you use it in the morning on rising and in the evening before sleeping.

I AM the Cosmic Diamond Violet Flame.

I AM the Law of Forgiveness for myself and all humanity.

I command that the entire monetary system on this planet be cleansed of all shadow energy, lack, limitation, scarcity, deprivation, and fear.

I AM free to fully receive the new faith currency now.

Add your own personal intense expectation to this decree if you'd like.

Your humble servant,

Saint Germain

12

Your Power Team

Beloved, come into my heart and let me hold you. Let me saturate you in the Love of the Divine Mother and the Provision of the Divine Father.

What we are bringing to you is nourishing provision through this time of transition.

We call it a new faith currency because it flows as a current of Pure Gold all around you, above you, below you, within your heart, and within Mother Earth.

As you welcome this 5th dimensional currency, it overrides the old 3rd dimensional system.

Keep focusing on where you are going, not the past

I want to introduce you to your Angels of Abundance power team today. They can help you in more ways than you can imagine.

Your team is your own Angel of Abundance, your own personal Dragon, and your personal Unicorn. They are all part of the Angelic Kingdom.

The Angels of Abundance serve on the 10th Dimension, the same sphere where you come daily to work in the Pure Gold

Project lab. They maintain the vibration of Pure Gold throughout the Universe. The 10th Dimension is their home.

Your own Guardian Angel opens the door to your Angel of Abundance. This beautiful Golden Angel of Abundance can help you lift into the frequency of Pure Gold whenever you ask and hold you there.

Dragons are cosmic guardians. They can travel between dimensions. They help to build and break up energy.

Your personal Dragon has been waiting for your call for a long time. Your personal Dragon can help you travel to the Temple of Gold Pyramid every day. They can help you call in other Dragons to assist you.

Unicorns are the purest of the pure. Everyone knew their personal Unicorn in Atlantis. They have come back in full force to help you and all of humanity and the Earth in this ascension process. A Unicorn is fully enlightened, and its third eye has become solid as a horn.

There are many Unicorns in my entourage. My personal Unicorn has been with me since the beginning of time, as has yours.

Your personal Unicorn is ready to serve you at the highest level. Ask this mighty being of light to touch its horn to your heart and your third eye with the spiritual technology of the new faith currency. It can also saturate all your chakras with Divine Light. It will flood you with the keys and light codes of Pure Gold, the new faith currency.

Remember your divine authority is the three-fold flame within your heart. Your I AM Presence is always directing. I Am Love. I Am Wisdom. I Am Will.

Take some time today to center in your Beloved I AM Presence, call Archangel Michael to surround you in Divine Protection, and connect and ground into the Earth.

One by one call in your power team. Start with your Angel of Abundance. Give some time to feel into Its presence and vibration.

Ask two simple questions. Pause to receive each answer and write it down in your journal.

"What shall I call you?"

"How can you assist me?

Call in your personal Dragon and ask the same questions.

Now call in your personal Unicorn and let this magnificent being of light touch your heart and then your third eye with its horn, to tune you in to its presence. Then ask the same questions.

Trust all that you receive and have fun with this.

The Angels of Abundance, the Dragons, and the Unicorns will always lift you up and refresh you and set you in the right direction.

I love and adore you,

Mother Mary and the Angels of Abundance

13

Rest in the Bounty

The new faith currency is a currency of Love. Love dissolves fear.

If you find yourself gathering worries about debt, the bills, and your future - STOP!

You can't afford to do that right now. It's an old mental habit that isn't helping you.

Take it easy and don't push against it. Give those worries over to your High Holy Self and ask your Angels of Abundance power team to help you dissolve this old habit.

Choose love instead. Find something you love and let it fill your heart and mind.

Ask your Unicorn to multiply this love and flood all your money with it. Flood your bank accounts, your investments, your wallet, savings, credit cards, debt, and bills with the bounty of Love.

This currency is not from the same root as working hard and then getting paid. This is Grace.

Rest in it. Allow the nourishing provision of the abundance, that belongs to you, to surround you like a cocoon and rest in the bounty.

Don't try to figure this all out in your mind. It's truly a download. The music is encoded with the new faith currency that's backed by Pure Gold.

As you go to bed tonight listen to the song, "Rest in the Bounty."
*

Rest in Grace tonight and we'll be working with you on this. Your entire Pure Gold Project team is with you every step of the way.

This is a currency of love. Your LOVE!

Always yours,

Manna

*"Rest in the Bounty" is on Jennifer's *Opulence EP*.

14

Drop of Gold

Beloved, come with me on a journey into the depths of your heart where only the Truth resides.

Center yourself in your heart, your Beloved I AM Presence. Take a moment to ground into the Earth and ask Archangel Michael to surround you in Divine Protection.

Allow your heart to connect with my Immaculate Heart. Use your breath to center into this Divine Union.

Withdraw your attention from the outer world. Let the attachments to what you think you know about your supply, your source of income, and where it comes from be dissolved as we sink deeper into your sacred heart.

It could be your stimulus checks, unemployment benefits, social security, your job, your spouse, your mutual funds and investments, or your savings. Anything else in this world that's trying to convince you that if you only had this . . . you'd be ok, and you'd be secure.

If only I had . . .

Let it all go.

As we sink deeper into your heart, see the brilliance of the dazzling White Light of Creation draw you in and saturate every part of your being, your thoughts, your feelings, your memories, your expectations, and disappointments.

Become the Light, simply the Light. Give way to it.

Now enter the Golden Sun in the center of your heart and be still.

Feel the full presence of the Christ Buddha Light only.

Say: *I joyfully accept that this is who I AM. I AM a Child of the Light.*

Right in the center of your heart is a drop of Pure Gold. It is from the Great Central Sun and was given to you from the Beloved Divine at the beginning of your eternal life.

I am placing my finger right on this drop of Pure Gold, Beloved, so you will awaken to it now.

There are more riches in this drop of Pure Gold than this world will ever have.

Feel that eternal connect with your endless supply. It comes with a promise. "You are always taken care of, every time, all the time. Every need will be met without question. You are a precious part of ME."

Drink that in Beloved. Your part in this promise is to trust and rely on the supply from Mother Father and let go of the outer. Let go of the need to 'get' anything from this world. This world is your schoolroom. It is not your supply. It gives you the opportunity to give your divine gifts.

The world needs your divine gifts NOW. Your gift of LOVE is the most powerful gift you can give at this time.

Do not be afraid to love unconditionally, knowing that you are always supplied by this drop of Pure Gold within the center of your heart.

I love and adore you,

Mother Mary and the Angels of Abundance

15

The Circle

Beloved, take some time today to honor your relationship with Mother Earth. Give thanks for all that she has provided for you.

Look at the nature that surrounds you. Bless it and give thanks for its nurturing beauty.

Give thanks for the provision of food on your table and the water that you drink.

The entire elemental Kingdom is here to serve you. Honor them by acknowledging and blessing them.

You are an intimate part of this cosmic dance, Beloved. See it as a circle of Life that's continuously moving. You receive the gifts of the Earth and return the blessing of thanksgiving.

Whatever you give comes back to you on this circle of Life. It's a Universal Law. You can never out give the Universe.

Beloved, I'm asking you to fully receive the new faith currency and keep it moving in the circle of Life.

Take some time to center in your I AM Presence, your Monad. Ground into the Earth and stand in the center of your 12 x 12 Sacred Geometry. Feel the expansion of your full Eternal Self.

Ask the Angels of Abundance to join you and magnify this activity.

Speak out loud:

I am the perfect symmetry of 12 x 12. I am complete. All 144 aspects of my being are here, secured in one place now. I AM fully functioning as the sovereign creator blueprint, I AM. I AM the Currency of Light. I AM the Currency of Love. I AM the Currency of Pure Gold. I AM, that I AM!

See the Golden Mist starting to move from the drop of Gold within your heart. See it moving through your hands.

Now lavishly give it to the Earth and the Elemental Kingdom as a blessing of the new faith currency. See it flowing through the air, the water, the ground, and through the rays of the Sun, saturating everything.

Shower it through your neighborhood and see all the people and animals receiving the new faith currency.

Use your imagination as you continue sending it into the structures and systems of the world. See it flowing through the cell towers, the electrical lines, and all communication systems. See it in the halls of government and education. See it filling up all healing and faith centers around the world.

Keep going until the entire Earth is covered in Golden Mist.

Take a big breath and pause.

Feel the Golden Mist coming back to you on the circle of Life and lavishly receive the riches of Heaven.

Beloved, you have been of great service to the new faith currency today.

I love and adore you,

Mother Mary and the Angels of Abundance

"The Circle" (on *lie down in that grass* CD)

By Jennifer Ruth Russell

The Circle, the Circle goes round and round

What goes round comes round again

The Circle, the Circle goes round and round

As it was in the beginning will never end

The Earth remembers and she's reminding me

The Law of the Circle is our ancestry

Remember she said when there was no doubt

You loved to give and give and give

And we never ran out

The Circle, the Circle goes round and round

What goes round comes round again

The Circle, the Circle goes round and round

As it was in the beginning will never end

Grandmothers, Grandmothers tell us again

Bout' the law of the circle that never ends

Give to the world the seeds of your life

And be willing to receive an abundant supply

The Circle, the Circle goes round and round

What goes round comes round again

The Circle, the Circle goes round and round

As it was in the beginning will never end

16

God of Gold

"Gold is the lodestone of Alpha and Omega." ~ God of Gold *

Dear one, I have been calling your name for centuries. Open your heart to me. I'm here to help you bring in the new faith currency in Light and Joy.

When Jennifer called to me, I appeared as the face of Santa Clause in the clouds. Many people see me that way. I love to laugh, and I am jolly. I bring Gold to the Earth.

You are entering into the Age of Aquarius, the Age of Miracles, a Golden Age.

Every Golden Age is backed by the substance of Pure Gold. The standard of gold is the Christ/Buddha consciousness. It is the golden rule fully expressed.

"Gold is precipitated sunlight for the balance of the mind and the emotions and the flow of life even in the physical temple." *

The rivers and veins of Gold that are found in the Earth are evidence of the Cosmic Beings of Light that have physically visited at one time or another. Bringing the Christ/Buddha consciousness they naturally carry with them.

You are remembering how to do this now. You are a Christed Buddha Being. Your three-fold flame within your heart makes it so.

As you are bringing in the new faith currency, make sure that you are wearing some gold on your body and have some in your home.

The gold acts like a focused magnet from the Great Central Sun, the home of Alpha and Omega and the Source of all Life, to you.

Always see my presence joyfully pouring the very substance of Gold into your lab time and affirmations.

There is a huge desire for the Pure Glory (Gold) of the Great Central Sun to be everywhere on Earth and in the lives of all humans. There is a Divine mandate for Gold to fulfill Its Divine Purpose on Earth. Its Divine Purpose is the Purity of Christ/Buddha Consciousness everywhere and within the hearts and minds of everyone. And for the use of expanding the Kingdom/Queendom of Heaven.

Focus on this Light coming right from the Great Central Sun. Call on me, the God of Gold to help flood it through your body and into your activities into the Earth. Listen for my laughter and laugh with me as we distribute this gift everywhere.

Speak out loud often:

I AM the Presence of Pure Gold. I command it here now.

Start thinking of Christ/Buddha Consciousness as Pure Gold. The two shall be made ONE for they already are. As above so below.

Forever yours,

God of Gold

Masters and Their Retreats, Mark and Elizabeth Prophet, Summit Lighthouse Publishing

17

Crystals

I am Constance. I have been with Jennifer for over 15 years. I am a raw citrine crystal. I am a teacher, a companion, a guide, a portal, and a powerful force field of Light.

I am grateful to be speaking with you today. I have been an intimate part of the Pure Gold Project from the very beginning. I am holding the new faith currency in Jennifer's auric field constantly. That's why she calls me Constance. I truly love that name.

The Crystal Kingdom is everywhere throughout this Solar System. We are within the Earth holding Divine Light. We hold ancient secrets, keys, and light codes within our bodies. We are protected and directed by the highest order of the Angelic Realm, the Seraphim. Currently, we are releasing more and more of our gifts.

As elementals we are divine energy. We are designed to work with you in expanding the new faith currency.

Assign a crystal to this Pure Gold Project.

Cleanse your crystal daily, as we pick up energy from the environment. You can use plain water, a sacred elixir, burning sage, or a prayer. Keep your crystal on your altar. Any sacred place in your home is fine.

Please keep us away from any arguments, harsh words, violence, and the broadcasting of any turmoil, aka as news. We love to go outside for a moon bath once a month to be recharged by the elements, trees, and the Angels.

Whenever you go to the lab to calibrate and re-calibrate bring your crystal along.

You are the container of the new faith currency. Your crystal will not only amplify your cellular healing as you receive the Light Codes, but it will also store the frequency of an Opulence Infusion. As you build the momentum, we will hold it for you and continually surround you in it.

Think of us as your team on the ground. Because you are a conductor of divine energy you can ask all your crystals, and the crystals in the Earth beneath you, to carry and increase the new faith currency for you and the world.

If you want to really amplify your experience in the lab, do so.

Call in your Angels of Abundance power team and the entire Pure Gold Project team.

As you take your seat in your calibration chamber; place a crystal between your feet, one behind you, your special assigned crystal in your left hand and another in your right hand.

You have made a simple, yet powerful diamond to contain and hold the calibration for you.

As you use your crystals, we also increase our Light. We may look like small stones and gems, but our etheric bodies are larger than your physical body.

We love working with you in building the new spiritual tools of the new divine earth.

Thank you for all that you are doing.

Shining in Love,

Constance

18

Go Beyond

You can never fail. The world is set up so that you will continually be in the checks and balances of what you came here to master. The choice will always be yours.

Hear me, Child of the Light, you can never fail. I AM Saint Germain.

You said, "Yes" to my invitation many lifetimes ago, to be a part of this giant leap into the 5th dimension while in a body.

You've spent a lot of time cleansing and healing, preparing for this moment. Now I'm asking you to enter the unknown.

Most of humanity has no idea how important they are as co-creators in the Light.

You are on the ground. You are the hands and feet, the very heart and mind of the Beloved Divine. You are constantly creating with your feelings and thoughts.

Now it's time to step into your true place and join with us in partnership. Right where you are is perfect. You aren't required to have transcended every difficulty to work with us.

I AM leading this Age of Freedom and Justice, with my Beloved, Lady Portia. All the Ascended Masters, Archangels, and Cosmic

Beings in the Galactic Council of Light are continually looking for your desire to be of service.

We are eager to bring in innovative ideas and solutions in every part of life on Earth.

Let your mind be open to receiving the divine ideas that will propel humanity forward. This will come through your heart's desire and your life lessons and experience.

What is important to you? What would you like to see change for the better on Earth? What could other people, in your same situation, use right now?

The journey of mastering financial lack and unworthiness in Jennifer's life is the force that propelled the Opulence Infusion, a new faith currency.

Her insistence for a new system of exchange and wealth for herself and all Lightworkers allowed us an opening to build a new faith currency with you, now.

Spend some time today seeing all your needs completely met. You don't have to work by the sweat of your brow any longer. Everything is taken care of.

Now what? Go beyond my friend. What can we create together?

Ask often, *'What is the optimum possibility in this situation?'* And listen for the answer.

You are a Child of the Light, and you can never fail. Walk out on the skinny branches. We'll meet you there.

Your Humble Servant,

Saint Germain

19

Be strong

Beloved, be strong and of good courage. *

We are asking you to step into the unknown with faith and bravery.

There are plenty of distractions all around you.

The wanting, needing, longing for a magical quick fix, is a strong pull for humanity.

We are calling you to step into an eternal and everlasting current of Abundance that never ends.

Every opening of Abundance in your life, is an awakening in your consciousness. Every new system is built by right of consciousness. It is a universal law.

Every time that you reach deeper into your connection with your Beloved, I AM Presence for your supply, you are building your consciousness and your faith currency.

Stop looking outside yourself for a fix.

As the world currencies move and change, continually go deeper in this relationship, and trust. As the banking systems begin to fail, the river of fear and panic will rage and overflow its banks.

Stay strong and ask the question often. "Is this fear/thought mine or am I picking it up from someone else?"

If it is your fear. Don't ignore it and hope it will go away. Face it head on and command your freedom. Every fear is an illusion. Even if it is a fear that has been with you for a long time and feels real.

Step into your divine authority and command its release in Divine Love.

Remember you are dismantling the old money system of lack, fear, deprivation, and scar-city within you.

Your faith currency will flow no matter what is going on in the outer world. It will keep you fully supplied and at peace. You will be helping others to stay in their calm as well, just by being with them.

Don't listen to the false promises of this system or that. Much of what you are hearing is still filled with manipulation and greed. These promises are not of the Christ Light.

Stay within, Beloved, and use your discernment. Ask us to help you see the Truth. We have a much higher perspective.

You will always be led by your impeccable guidance system. Listen daily, the voice within is a subtle voice.

Sometimes you will be led into challenging situations. This is to increase your faith and your reliance on your High Holy Self. These situations also help you release old patterns that are holding you back.

You have a natural self-correcting mechanism. Rejoice and give thanks for it.

Embrace your challenges. They are your invitation to step into choice and mastery.

This is your path into 5th dimensional living. You are stepping into your sovereign power, your ascension.

Remember we are your partners every step of the way. We can't do your work for you. We can help you, guide you, empower you, and cheer you on.

Your relationship with us will ease the journey. Rise into the joyful light, the magical presence, of our partnership.

We love and adore you,

Mother Mary and the Angels of Abundance

*"Be strong and of a good courage, fear not, nor be afraid of them: for the Lord thy God, he it is that doth go with thee; he will not fail thee, nor forsake thee." Deuteronomy 31:6

20

Declare

DECLARE: to proclaim, announce, make known, state, communicate, articulate, pronounce, express, broadcast, promulgate, trumpet.

I AM Archangel Michael, the Prince of Angels and the Defender of your Faith. My Beloved Lady Faith and I are the Archangels on the 1st Ray of sapphire blue. It is the Father Ray of will, faith, courage, bravery, provision, and protection.

The creative power of the 1st Ray is in your throat chakra. We are the Guardian Archangels of this creative center.

I'm grateful to share with you today the power of your voice and your declaration.

Every time you use your voice you are creating. However, when you deliberately declare something out loud, backed by your belief and faith, it is a powerful directive.

You are a magnet, a focus point, a station of creation on Earth. When you make the call, your call is answered, right where you are.

You are moving energy with your voice. When you declare and decree, you make it so.

If you repeatedly make a declaration, you are building and forming a new pattern, a new reality.

An affirmation, a decree, or an Empowered Prayer is a declaration. *

Always begin with the two most powerful words in the Universe, "I AM."

This immediately activates your Monad, your Beloved I AM Presence, the 12 x 12 powerhouse of your very existence. It is your divine authority.

Your declaration can be short or long. The one ingredient that makes it strong is the way the words make you feel. Do you feel powerful saying them? Do they lift you up? Do they benefit the world?

A good decree will activate all your subtle bodies and make you feel that the entire Universe is at your attention.

Take the time to create a decree for your new faith currency that feels powerful to you. Make it your own and speak it out loud daily. Ask Lady Faith and me to help you.

The Angels of Abundance will expand your declaration and I will protect and sustain it.

We've asked Jennifer to share the Abundance for Lightworkers decree that she has been using to help you get started.

Powerful One, what will you declare?

Thank you for helping us bring in this new spiritual technology of faith currency.

In love and faith,

Archangel Michael and Lady Faith

The Defenders of your faith

Abundance for all Lightworkers Decree

Beloved Mighty I AM Presence, in the name of my Holy Christ Self and by the love, wisdom and power of my threefold flame, I call forth the action of an Opulence Infusion, a new practical form of faith currency of Love Light, limitlessness, and Abundance, by the fire of my being, multiplied by the Flame of Precipitation, multiplied by the Golden Ray of all Supply, multiplied by the Cosmic Diamond Violet Flame, multiplied by the Fire of the Great Central Sun, and the Great Central Sun Magnet, multiplied by the Angelic Hosts Sacred Fire, Love and the Seven Mighty Elohim and their Divine Complements.

I call for the action of financial liberation, a new paradigm of Golden Prosperity on behalf of all Lightworkers and places that we gather.

I call for that power of the Flame I invoke and all that I AM to go forth now to bring financial Abundance, a new Golden Age, an Opulence Infusion, a new form of Faith currency, to all Lightworkers and Centers of Praise. I hold high all Practitioners and Artists of Healing Light, and all centers of fellowship where the Light is active.

I call the Earth and Fire Dragons into action to cleanse the Earth and the elementals of all lack, greed, oppression, power over others, all war, violence, depravity, and limitation, throughout all ley lines and the atmosphere. Continue to do so until our

Beloved Earth has been completely set free of causes and cores of man's deprivation. Thank you.

I call on the Golden 5th dimensional Dragons and the Light of the Golden White Unicorns of the 10th Sphere to infuse the Opulence of God throughout all of mankind, with a new faith currency of Christ Light, setting us free to experience Abundance as never before. Thank YOU.

I decree it in the name of my own Feminine Christhood, in the name of my own Ascended Master who I shall be and who I AM already.

For the seed is within itself and the seed of my Mighty 'I AM' Presence is with me in my heart. Therefore, I dedicate those percentages allowed me by the Fire of my life stream to the financial liberation and the precipitation of a new spiritual technology, a practical faith currency of Love Light for all. All needs met, POGO.

I call on Archangel Michael and the Angelic Host to permanently protect this word and activity of Life and keep it sustained invincible, always protected with the Prevention Flame.

This I do in the name of the Father, and of the Christ Child, and of the Holy Spirit, and of the Universal Divine Mother. I command Victory of Pure GOLD Pure God Supply NOW. I accept it done this hour in FULL POWER by the blessings of the Lords of Karma. In God's most Holy Name, I AM.

Empowered Prayer by Jennifer Ruth Russell and Mother Mary. This book will help you find your sovereign voice and be empowered to speak from it. It's available on Amazon.

21

Where we're going

Beloved, we adore you. We see you. We see where you are in your own individual path toward financial freedom. You represent many who are in the same place as you are today.

Where you've been and where you are going is the experience that brings in the new faith currency, which is powerful grist for this mill we're creating.

Thank you for being an open heart of receptivity with your feet on the ground, anchoring the new faith currency.

We love working in partnership with you. We have completed the first phase of pulling this new spiritual technology into the world through you.

Phase One has been establishing the scaffolding, the sacred geometry with light songs, that transmits the essence of Pure Gold on a new level for all of humanity.

You may think you didn't do enough. That is not true. You've done your part perfectly. You made it to Chapter 21.

In the last 21 chapters, you have healed lack on a cellular level through all your lifetimes and timelines. You've dismantled the old money fears and stories within you.

Your container, your faith, has become stronger every day. We see it glowing as a small golden sun in your auric field. It's picking up momentum and volume every day.

As we move into Phase Two, we want to continue anchoring your container of faith in your community of Light workers.

When you do this work together, combined with our assistance, we become a powerful force field of constructive change. We are your Galactic team of Pure Gold.

Phase Two of the Pure Gold Project will bring this technology into practical use. It will show up in ways that will blow your mind.

This currency will appear in unexpected ways. It may come to you as pliable sheets of iridescent gold (or a different form) that you can mold into any physical requirement of the hour, with your mind.

It may just appear in your bank account.

The Golden Mist is real. As you continue to POGO and experiment with it more and more, you'll see it transform into all needs met, right before your eyes.

The new faith currency will help create solutions for the big problems of the world. It will help to bring equality and honor to marginalized communities. It will house the homeless. It will heal the sick. It will help to dissolve and dismantle the systems of power that use and abuse people, animals, and the environment. It will bring the education system into compassion, creativity, and earth wisdom. Children will be encouraged to develop their divine faculties. It will nourish and change mankind's relationship with the Elemental Kingdom, which will create beauty everywhere. It will provide the funds for big change in the world.

You are part of these incredible co-creations that build the new divine earth.

Since this is a currency of consciousness, it can only be used through a pure heart and egoless mind.

Therefore, Phase One is important and will continue to be so.

Be dedicated to your daily spiritual practice and re-calibration. It will keep you on track and up to speed with where we are going next.

Stay in community and activities of Light.

And always stay connected to my Immaculate Heart. I am a reflection of you.

I love and adore you,

Mother Mary and the Angels of Abundance

Part Two

Let's Get Practical

22

Sacred Fire

Every morning when you calibrate in the very essence of the new faith currency and infuse in Opulence you are filled with it. Your intention to calibrate and re-calibrate is enough. You are ready to go.

You are ready to move this energy of Opulence anywhere. This is yours to do, to conduct and move Divine Energy.

When you are feeling weak and vacillating, call my name and ask me to fill up every electron in your auric field with my Presence.

You are part of me as I am part of you. Lean into this truth that there is no upper or lower, not here or anywhere, there is only One Life. You are a part of this Life as much as I AM.

You are powerful. Your word is directive and influences the movement of the Sacred Fire.

Try this now. Notice your energy level and speak out loud. "I AM Metatron." three times.

You have called the Sacred Fire, my Golden Orange Ray, the 12 X 12 sacred Geometry, and my very Presence into action.

Say my name again, three times, and feel the creative power within you start to increase. Now, do it one more time. Say my name three times.

Acknowledge that you are conduit of the new faith currency. *I AM a conduit of the Opulence of God. I call and command this Mighty Sacred Fire, the Currency of Love and Opulence, to flow into _____, _____, and _____.*

Keep calling on the Opulence of God to saturate everything. Start with your own life. See the new faith currency filling your bank account, your bills, your debt, your wallet, your food, and water.

Keep going seeing it move out throughout your area. Into your neighbors' homes, into the people living on the street, into schools, businesses, grocery stores, banks, clothing, drug, and hardware stores, and anything that comes to mind.

Go even farther and see it flooding throughout the elemental kingdom and the nature spirits. Bless the water moving through all the natural springs, rivers, and oceans. Then follow the distribution systems of water, see the Sacred Fire moving throughout every home and building.

Conduct it through the soil and all the microscopic life within it, the elementals, the mineral, and crystal kingdoms.

See it gently filling up the sky with ribbons of Pure Gold.

See the Golden mist sprinkling around every animal, bird, and all life in the waters.

When you feel complete with your conducting, end with a simple and powerful statement.

I AM Metatron, I AM, that I AM, and I command an Opulence Infusion, a new faith currency, be permanently established throughout the Earth, now. I give thanks. It is done. And so, it is.

Get used to commanding, my friend. Without your command the Sacred Fire can't descend from the higher octaves. You have the privilege of calling it into the electrons that make up all of life on Earth.

Keep on. You are remembering how powerful you really are.

I AM with you always,

Metatron

23

Walk with Us

We are the Angels of Abundance. Our entire job is to flow the God supply of all that is Good to mankind and the Elemental Kingdom.

We respond wherever we are called with this glorious gift of the Beloved Divine.

This gift is not limited in any way. The only limitation is within your mind and your experience.

We want you to see this gift, the flow of Abundance, the new faith currency, as real. It is more real than the thoughts within your mind and the historic experience that humanity keeps dragging along.

The past money story looks like old, outdated baggage that has nothing of value. It's time to throw it in the cosmic trash bin of the Violet Flame. You are the only one that can make that decision.

We suggest that you do it now.

You are not your past. You are a sovereign being and can decide what you'd like to carry forward and what you'd like to leave behind. You are not your families' beliefs or habits. Your true inheritance is only Abundance.

We suggest that you take time often to call on us.

Let's take time to love each other and to commune together.

See us surrounding you with a bubble of Golden White Mist, Pure Creator Light.

Step into this bubble completely. Breathe it in to your lungs and fill your heart.

Let us fill up every cell in your body and your mind. Keep breathing in our Presence and Radiation into your being.

Let yourself let go of any gripping and holding on.

Relax in our Love. Feel the edges of where you think you end and we begin start to dissolve, as we become One.

Take your time with us.

Open yourself to hear our voice.

Ask the question: *How can I use you in ways that I haven't thought of yet?*

Write down everything that you hear.

Let us participate in your experience of the new faith currency.

You can keep this bubble around you as you go about your day. Keep walking and talking with us.

We are here for you.

We love and adore you,

The Angels of Abundance

24

Financial Healing

Beloved, you are going through a financial healing.

The beautiful Emerald Green Ray that I, Archangel Raphael, radiate is a Flame of Illumined Truth, Healing, Manifestation and Music.

It is designed perfectly for your financial healing.

Let's begin with the Illumined Truth about you. Truth makes everything simple.

Your divine inheritance is Opulence.

As you accept this Truth and make it your own, you begin to heal all the places within you that believe something different.

The Truth sets you free. Free to create. Free to receive miracles.

The habits within the mental body make up entire scenes of fear and panic, which causes you to clutch, grasp, and try to hold on to the little that you feel you have.

Holding on to lack creates a lot of tension and stress in your body temple.

Use the Truth to heal your mental Body.

Speak out loud:

My divine inheritance is Opulence. I claim it now. I command all thoughts of lack to release now. I AM the Opulence of the Beloved Divine.

Your emotional body stores feelings of non-safety and turmoil which sends your nervous system whirling. This can keep you feeling powerless. The emotional surge is in constant motion.

A state of non-safety and turmoil also affects your physical body and keeps you from resting, restoring, and letting go in trust.

You are the divine authority of your emotional body. Use the Truth to heal it.

Calm down this undulating body by singing a simple lullaby to yourself.

Gentle wrap your arms around yourself, see the Emerald Green Ray surrounding you, and sway as if comforting a baby.

Make up a simple child light melody with these words. The music will heal you.

I AM loved. I AM safe. I AM held in the arms of Divine Love and Abundance.

I AM loved. I AM safe. I AM whole. I AM always cared for. I let go and rest in this Truth.

Your etheric body records everything. It doesn't know how to discern what is beneficial to you and what is not. It contains the memories of all your lifetimes. I urge you to take dominion of this body now.

The ancient memories of money trauma are in your etheric body. You have the power to cleanse your memory body.

Set up a healing program to do this work during your sleep time.

Before you sleep, connect with your Beloved I AM Presence, your Pure Gold Project team, Archangel Zadkiel, Holy Amethyst, Mother Mary, and Me. Ask for our assistance as you sleep to cleanse your etheric body.

Speak the following out loud:

Beloved etheric body, I am no longer interested in any memories of trauma, lack, scarcity, or deprivation. I command my wholeness. I call for a complete healing and transmutation of these memories during my sleep time. I ask that you only record memories that are in alignment with my divine inheritance. I AM the Opulence of God. I AM always nurtured and provided for. I declare the Truth. I AM free. I am thankful. And so it is. In God's most Holy Name, I AM.

The cells of your physical body have responded to your declarations in word and song.

You have claimed the Illumined Truth of your divine inheritance.

The more you do claim your divine inheritance, manifesting the new faith currency will become easier for you.

I AM the Way, the Truth, and the Life.

Always at your service,

Archangel Raphael

25

Your Body Elemental

I am your connection to all that is physical and magical. I am your Body Elemental. I have been with you since the very beginning.

Through all your lifetimes I've crafted your physical body from the divine blueprint given to me from your Holy Christ Self. I was there weaving together the very fibers of your high heart with Beloved Mother Mary when you were in the womb.

I then became the caretaker of your body temple. I also take care of all your subtle bodies; your etheric, mental, emotion, and physical body.

As your Guardian Angel is the key to open the door to the Angelic Kingdom. I hold the key to opening the Elemental Kingdom for you.

Our partnership is important for our Ascension. I am ascending too.

I am an advanced Elemental. I trained for centuries to become a Body Elemental. I belong to a soul family of Body Elementals.

As an Elemental I am influenced by your vibration. You have the divine authority, through your thoughts, your words, and feelings, to direct me.

Every cell of your body, and every atom of your auric field is listening to you, the Beloved I AM.

Our relationship will help you in manifesting the new faith currency and building the divine new earth.

I'm asking you to get to know me. Give me a name. Take the time to acknowledge me, let me give you my vast wisdom, and give me loving direction.

I am the head of your Elemental team. Yes, you have an entire team of 12 Elementals that are here to serve you and to help you come back into cooperation and harmony with the Elemental Kingdom.

The Pure Gold Project is made up of every Kingdom.

We are the part of the Company of Heaven that will help you pull the high frequency, the very essence of Pure Gold to the Earth. Every precious gem and nugget of precious metal has been found on the Earth.

Consciously walk with me daily and let's open your powerful connection to the magical world of nature, built by the Elementals. Our entire service is to the One Light of Source.

"The Earth is the Beloved Divine's, and the fullness thereof,

the world and all who dwell therein." Psalm 24:1

At your service,

Your Body Elemental

(Through *Morning Glory*, Jennifer's Body Elemental)

To fight the body elemental is useless; to pamper it, is to lose it. To become acquainted with it IN THE MATURE DIGNITY OF THE MASTER OF THE HOUSEHOLD, WHEN REQUIRED TO DIRECT HIS

IMMEDIATE STAFF, IS WISDOM. — *"21 Essential Lessons, Vol. 1"*
by Werner Schroeder

26

Quiet Intimacy

Beloved, as you are receiving a new faith currency, a new way of living in the 5th dimension, you are being calibrated to a new frequency.

Calibration requires a lot of quiet, stillness and space. Don't fill up your entire calendar right now. You need time to be in the silence.

There are many voices talking. In the news, in social media, and in the ascension community.

Knowledge and information will push you into overload at this time.

We're asking you to turn down the volume of those voices and come within.

Allow the voice of your own I AM Presence to have your full attention now. Allow it to be the only voice that you listen to.

Start where you are. Schedule time with your Beloved. Light a candle. Slow down your breath, let your heart open and connect.

Come into the divine union of your heart and stay there.

Be simple. It is your Love. Come into the intimacy of this love affair as a radical and attentive lover.

Give yourself permission to nurture this love.

Your Beloved will nourish and supply you every day. It will bring the wisdom and guidance to make the best choices. It will inspire you into action in perfect timing.

This relationship is your supply and the answer to every desire of your heart. It is your path to your true wealth and abundance.

Everything else is secondary.

Give space and time to come into the quiet and be still.

The intimacy you share will seal the new light codes and the frequencies of the new faith currency into your entire being.

I love and adore you,

Mother Mary and the Angels of Abundance

27

Your Physical Body

Your physical body is an instrument of abundance. It is designed to receive the fullness of the Earth and all her gifts.

We want to help you receive the new faith currency in your body today.

Your experience of being a human divine on a free-will planet and in the density of the 3rd dimension is incredibly valuable. It builds your own personal treasure of mastery and the knowledge base of the entire human race.

Consciously ascending in a body is a giant experiment that you are proving right now.

Your body is the entrance point of life experience.

I want you to start seeing your body as a receiving vessel. All your other subtle bodies and 12 chakras are supporting your body. See your body as the trunk of the tree, so to speak.

I want to help you experience your body in a new way today.

Call my name and ask for my assistance.

Beloved Metatron, help me to experience my body today as a receiving vessel.

Ground into the Earth and feel yourself as an earthling.

As you read these words feel your eyes looking at the words and your mind understanding them.

Experience the breath starting to deepen, automatically embracing your body, and bringing it into a receptive and aligned state.

Take your time. Close your eyes for a few moments and feel the cells of your body. Feel them moving and responding to your attention. Open your heart and love the cells of your body.

Watch or feel into their response.

Ask them now to calibrate to the new faith currency frequency and see your entire team from the Pure Gold Project gently filling every cell with the Pure Gold Light of Opulence.

What does that feel like? Notice and keep going for a few minutes. Breathe and receive pure Opulence into the cells of your body.

Feel my Presence increasing, amplifying, and multiplying your experience.

Now command your Body Elemental, the director of your cells, to seal this Light within every cell, atom, and electron of your physical body and to keep it sustained.

I Am the new faith currency in my body. I Am a living and moving transformer and transmitter of the New Opulence codes. This is a joyful experience of Abundance.

I AM with you always,

Metatron

28

Our Partnership

Beloved, we are coming to you today as one voice.

We are your Opulence team. We are your partners in establishing the New Faith Currency in your life and on Earth.

We all have our specialties, and we operate as a highly efficient collective. You are part of this team.

Sometimes one of us will come into your awareness to help you focus on a certain aspect of your process. All of us are working with you every step of the way.

As in every healthy partnership, let's clarify our roles.

We are infusing you with the new spiritual technology, the light keys, and codes that you need to step up into the frequency of Opulence.

We are protecting your progress as you shed the old systems of beliefs that have been running you.

Your job is to focus on your desire.

Use your own will and insist, with intense expectation, for this new spiritual technology to be established within you and the Earth.

Daily call on us and ask for our help.

Your job is to consciously release the old ways that have limited you for centuries, into faith.

We magnify and multiply your efforts every time. Be patient with the process.

Every time you catch yourself in an old thought of lack, call on us to help you transmute it right then and there. Ask us to help you with a new thought of plenty.

Remember lack can show up in love, in time, in your giving and receiving, in your food choices, in your wallet, and in many other ways. It's insidious and has many cloaks of disguise.

Be honest with yourself and call lack what it is.

Ask for what you need.

We operate at a higher level of Light then you do. We can't do our part of this partnership without you.

You literally pull the Light Codes of Opulence to the Earth and establish them here.

Take the time to come into the Temple of Pure Gold to be with us. To calibrate and re-calibrate your vibrational frequency is important. This is our love time. It bonds and builds our partnership. It allows us to minister to you in ways beyond your own understanding at this time.

Don't hold out on our love time. It's essential for this project.

We are with you always. We are at the ready to assist you.

We love and adore you,

Your Opulence Team (Pure Gold Project Team)

29

Seeing with Archangel Raphael

Today's meditation is an active meditation with Archangel Raphael. Take some time to center and open your twelve chakras before you begin.

Beloved, let the third eye open your new faith currency even more.

Flow into the higher aspect of me with your intention. Come into my Radiation. We are One.

Now lift your third eye and join it with mine. Let us see together.

Envision the full picture of the new faith currency with me now.

Imagine a holographic image of the globe.

See light workers holding the pure gold essence throughout the planet. See them spreading the new faith currency through their daily interactions. Through their money interactions, spending and receiving through the exchange that now exists.

See the Opulence infusion fully saturating the new faith currency within the old. Take your time and breathe into this vision.

See the elementals that hold those forms of exchange dancing in delight. They are free to do Father Mother's work according to their design. See them bringing the nourishment, provision, and choice of the new faith currency into money.

Now see all greed dissolving and only the generosity of Spirit moving through the planet.

Keep visualizing wherever money is exchanged.

As we always tell you, make sure you infuse your own money with Opulence. See it coming and going in a river of plenty. A river of creativity. A river of healing, filled with joy, peace, provision, and love.

Now allow me to show you through my eyes, Beloved.

I see your light shining Opulence. It's glowing around you. It's filling up your home, your street, and the neighborhood. Your aura is calling us into action, and we are amplifying your light throughout the cosmos.

You are a beacon, a lighthouse of the new faith currency.

Thank you, Beloved.

Accept who you are. Love yourself completely. Believe in yourself and have faith.

Always at your service,

Archangel Raphael

30

Uncertainty

Uncertainty is the fertile ground that is birthing the new faith currency.

As the old structures are dissolving and the Divine New Earth is under construction, uncertainty will be a way of life.

Beloved, when you find that everything is uncertain, and you are feeling a bit wobbly in your faith. These are the moments that your faith has the opportunity to grow by leaps and bounds.

Saint Germain has given you this simple teaching that as you ascend you must walk through two doors, doubt and fear.

I'm inviting you today to see these two doors as an invitation to Love.

You don't need to wrestle down that which feels uncertain. You don't need to tackle your fear.

Acknowledge what you are feeling and then flow into loving yourself and that fear to the best of your ability.

We are always right here supporting you. Remember to call on us to assist you.

You are dismantling the strongholds of fear and all its extensions. Your habits of worry, anxiety, nervousness, analysis, dread, all the way to terror, are just fear dressing up in different clothing.

The answer is always love, Beloved. This is a currency of Love.

The crevices of your human mind are craving this Love Divine. The holes you feel in your heart are crying for IT. When you feel that you are not enough, you need to love that part of yourself tenderly.

Your Holy Christ Buddha Self is continually flowing the love of your Mighty I AM Presence to you. Your job is to use it and ask for it to be applied right where you need it.

Uncertainty is becoming the way of life on planet Earth. It is the way of Love and Faith. Do your best not to push against this river of uncertainty.

Anchor in that which is REAL. Your Beloved I AM Presence will never leave or forsake you. Never. It is always certain.

When you start to know faith in every electron of your being, you'll be resting in the bounty of always being cared for, provided for, guided, and loved no matter what.

Embrace the gift of uncertainty and see it as an invitation to your true liberation of Love.

See yourself as precious for this is who you truly are.

I love and adore you,

Mother Mary and the Angels of Abundance

31

Release the Burden

We know that this is an intense time of self-healing and transformation for everyone.

You are in the middle of the great shift as humanity is working through the 4th dimension into the 5th dimension.

You are consciously ascending. You are courageous. We are continually amazed at your fortitude and determination to take on your lessons and transmute the shadow into Light.

As a part of our team, we wanted to encourage you in what is yours to do, and what is not yours to do.

We feel the burden that many of you feel in making a living and making ends meet.

The vast magnificence of who you are wasn't created to 'make a living' for you are Life Itself. You are the Opulence of the Beloved Divine.

Today we are asking you to release the burden, this heaviness of your financial life. Give this burden to us. Put this burden on the platter of your faith and serve it up to us.

This burden is a pattern, a habit of thought that has gone on for centuries. It's time for it to be released, now.

What is your responsibility? Take a few minutes to write down your answer to this question in your journal.

If the Universe will always provide what you need, every moment of every day, what is yours to do?

Your job is to keep your heart open in faith, and to receive. To stay in a place of miracle readiness; to be available by forgiving yourself and everyone else of all mistakes; to keep your daily spiritual practice fresh and alive; to keep your heart pure and in harmony; to stay connected and in tune with your Beloved I AM Presence and with us, your Pure Gold Project team, and to insist on abundance, peace, and joy.

You are here as a director of Divine Energy. You are a conductor of the full spectrum of Light. Your three-fold flame is your divine authority. Look ahead and command what you need to be there. *

Remember you are the chooser, not the doer.

The burden of how your needs are met is not your job. It is the job of your Holy Christ Buddha Self, your Universal Manager. **

We invite you to create a new pattern, a new habit of thought.

I AM the open door that no one can shut, into the Great Opulence of God, made manifest in my hands and use. "I AM Discourses" Saint Germain

Thank you for being on our team.

We are with you always,

The Pure Gold Project Team

*The Three-fold flame is the garment of your Holy Christ Self. It is the Omnipotence (the Blue Flame of the Divine Masculine),

the Omniscience (the Illumined Wisdom of the Sunshine Yellow Ray), and the Omnipresence (the Transfiguring Unconditional Love of the Divine Feminine Crystal Pink Ray).

**Your Holy Christ Buddha Self is the wisdom of your soul, a step-down transformer of your Beloved I AM Presence.

32

Ask for More

I AM Lady Nada, the Goddess of Love, the Lady Master of the Ruby Gold Ray of Peace, Grace, and Service. I also serve on the Karmic Board and have many assignments in this Solar System.

Beloved, I want to encourage you to ask for more. We see you opening your cup of receiving little by little.

Hear me now, there is absolutely no limitation to what you may have. Nothing is withheld from you. I'm asking you today to release yourself from the old idea that you must earn Opulence. That you must check off an impossible list in order to have more.

Your Beloved I AM Presence is waiting for you to ask and command, and to receive more. This primary relationship, the Divine Union, your Holy Matrimony, is your Ascension. It is your Source, your Love, your Creative Power, your Super Intelligence, your ALL.

Close your eyes and visualize the infinite flow of Opulence that comes from your Beloved. Notice if you perceive the flow as a small trickle or a full gushing waterfall.

You can open this flow even more, as you would a faucet. There's nothing holding back this flow except your own ideas of limitation, and they can be changed.

Up level your asking, Beloved. Begin to command and demand that more of the flow of Opulence open for you in ways that you can use in your life.

Beloved Presence I AM, you are my Mastery, my ALL. I love and adore you. I'm asking for more Abundance to flow in my life now. I command an endless supply of money and the new faith currency come to me easily. I demand that what I have in my possession now be multiplied a thousand times. Thank you. And so it is. Beloved I AM.

When you receive money in any form, immediately turn your attention to your Beloved I AM Presence. Give thanks and picture this supply coming to you from your only Source. Now ask for more and picture the flow growing. Enthusiastically command that the money you have just received increase a thousand times.

I know that commanding and demanding may feel too strong for many of you. I am giving you these words and instructions because many of you are waiting and hoping that something will happen. You're keeping your supply outside of yourself, from other sources. Treat this relationship as you would a human relationship, not wanting to be too pushing or demanding.

These words will not only strengthen your asking, but they will also put you in right alignment with your Divine Inheritance. Your Beloved I AM Presence is waiting for your command.

"Ask and you will receive" is real, Beloved. Take your rightful place of being a fully endowed Light Being, a Master.

Try it this week and see what happens. The evidence that you receive will be your greatest teacher.

I am always at your service. Call on me to assist you to be stronger in your asking.

I Am Yours,

Lady Nada

33

Stay Alert

I AM Mighty Victory, the tall man from Venus. My petition to the Karmic Board was granted and the Occult Law, which had governed the Mystery Schools for 80,000 years, was dissolved. The dissolution allowed everyone to receive the teachings in simple ways so that you could understand them and use them.

I am here to assist Saint Germain during this time of Ascension on Earth. I am on the Pure Gold Project team to continuously remind you that you are always the Victorious Presence of the Mighty I AM.

Beloved, the new faith currency is active now.

There is no time in Spirit. Yesterday, today, and tomorrow is an illusion. There is only the powerful now.

This spiritual technology is for your use immediately.

We're asking you to stay alert to where you are placing your attention. Is your attention on Opulence and is your feeling following your attention? If not, bring it back into the flow of the Golden Mist.

Your Beloved I AM Presence, the Giver of your Supply, is your Source. Think of what you need in this moment. Your responsibility is to choose your experience and make the call. Stay in harmony with your choice.

Call on the Golden Ray of Infinite Abundance, Eternal Peace, and the God Supply of all that is Good. Direct this Golden Ray physically and practically into what you require, right now.

Even if you lost everything yesterday and only have one penny to hold in your hand, there is no limitation to what you can receive today. There's no time and space in Spirit and there's no judgement about where you are.

Simply make the call and command your Beloved I AM Presence to provide and then let it go. Stay alert to where you are placing your attention.

The responsibility of your I AM Presence is to do the rest. IT is the action that moves the Mighty Rays, the Divine currents and currency to where it is needed.

Even as you are cleansing the ancient feelings of unworthiness and un-deservedness, and the traumatized memories of lack … ALL IS YOURS. VICTORY IS YOURS. Don't wait to make the call and command.

The only thing you need to heal is the pain of separation. There is no God outside of you. There is nothing or no one in this world that will provide for you. You were designed perfectly to tap into the reservoirs of the Universe through your Beloved I AM Presence.

Stay alert, my friend.

In this moment are you connected and communing with your Beloved? Are you allowing yourself time for your spiritual practice, your love time?

Give way to this Divine Union for it is your ALL. Let your Beloved I AM Presence flow the new faith currency through you, starting right now.

A good question to ask yourself often is *Am I in the flow of Opulence right now?*

You are always Victorious.

I AM Mighty Victory,
At your service

Part Three

The Golden White Unicorns

34

The Golden White Unicorns

You've come to earth at a magical time of big change. It's a time of remembering of your Eternal Soul Self. It's a time of stepping into your divine sovereignty bringing all your lifetimes of training into fruition.

The full use of your divine faculties will help you to fulfill your divine mission.

Yes, you came here on a divine mission. It is the fixed design of your Eternal Self, your Monad, your I AM.

My name is Thom. I AM a Unicorn. I am a part of a collective of Golden White Unicorns from the 10th Sphere. We are part of your Pure Gold Project team. We have been with you in different forms since the time of Lemuria.

I have been Jennifer's personal Unicorn since that time. You also have a personal Unicorn.

Because you are part of the Opulence Infusion, the new faith currency that is being manifest on Earth right now, your Unicorn is also here as a part of this powerful collective.

We've asked Mother Mary and Jennifer to give us the opportunity to speak to you now and strengthen our partnership. We desire to assist you to Ascend in Opulence and Beauty.

The Angels and the Dragons help you through your heart center. The Dragons are especially helping you to dismantle and clear the old belief systems on the earth plane. We are here to help you on a soul level and to fulfill your deepest desire.

We're asking you to begin by feeling into our Presence. We hold the highest frequency of Purity and Opulence. Your soul will recognize us immediately.

We are now in the 7th to 12th dimension. We are etheric and come in many shapes and forms. Your experience with us will be unique.

Many of you will recognize our horse-like nature. We choose this strong shape with the Galactic Counsel of Light when we incarnated on Earth. Our brow chakra, our horn of Pure Light, is where we direct and radiate the Divine Rays. *

Many Unicorns are now coming back into Earth's sphere and the awareness of mankind to help during this magical time of great change.

As you turn your attention to your soul mission and to us, especially your personal Unicorn, ask the question? "What is possible?" Be open to receive the answers that are beyond your human mind.

I look forward to this journey together.

Always at your service,

Thom the Unicorn

*Read more about our history in the *"Magic of the Unicorns"* by Diana Cooper.

35

Worry or Opulence

Beloved, come into my heart. Bring with you every bit of worldly currency that is in your possession right now. Put it right here on the altar of our divine union.

Enter the fullness of your Lightbody, Your Beloved I AM Presence. Feel into the Brilliant White Light of your Presence and lift with me into the 10th Sphere of Pure Gold.

Feel my Immaculate Heart calibrating your heart to its Perfection. Remember Abundance flows through our Immaculate Hearts, Beloved.

As we enter the Temple of Pure Gold bring all your present financial wealth to the altar of this Temple. *

Release your money from your physical, mental, emotional, and etheric bodies.

Lift up only as a Lightbody into the Golden Mist of Opulence.

See this mist rising through the Sacred Geometry of 12 X 12. ** See your 12 - 5th Dimensional Chakras spinning counterclockwise cleansing all essence of lack and worry. Take your time. The Angels of Abundance with Archangel Zadkiel, Holy Amethyst, and Archangel Gabriel are assisting you in releasing the old records of scarcity and deprivation.

As you reach your Stellar Gateway connect once more with your I AM Presence, your Monad, and make your command.

I AM the Divine Authority of my life. I Am no longer interested in spending my precious life energy worrying about my financial life. I surrender it completely to you, Beloved. You are the only Source of my Supply, and we are One. I command a continuous infusion of Opulence to now take over. I command the Pure Gold Project team to assist me in staying in the high vibration of Opulence every moment of my life. Thank you. It is DONE!

Now see the Golden White Unicorns in a Brilliant White circle above you. In unison they blaze Pure Opulence directly to you.

Move this column with your breath in a clockwise motion.

Breath it down from your Beloved Presence's portal, your Stellar Gateway chakra and let it saturate into your Soul Star Chakra, move down through your Causal Chakra and now through your Crown Chakra, your Third Eye Chakra, your Throat, and into your Heart.

As you breathe in Opulence with the Golden White Unicorns feel your Heart expand. Now allow it to flow through your Solar Plexus Charka, Your Naval Chakra, Your Sacral Chakra, and your Root Chakra flooding a foot beneath your feet into your Earth Star Chakra.

Ask Archangel Sandalphon to secure this infusion permanently into your Earth Star Chakra.

As you turn your attention now to the altar in the Temple of Gold, look at your current wealth. Bless it. Pour your love into it. See it shining in the White Gold Light. Speak tenderly to it and ask it to multiply.

As we gently come back to your current now, do your best, Beloved, to keep your mental body, your mind, only on Opulence. The old habit of worry is released. It has no power over you.

Choose Opulence every day, Beloved, and love your money. Be at one with your money, it is preparing for the big change that is coming.

I love and adore you,

Mother Mary and the Golden White Unicorns

*Chapter 1 - Calibration

** Chapter 7 - Sacred Geometry

36

Unicorn Blessings

The Unicorns are often thought of as mythical creatures from another time. Let me tell you, they are real. They are here now and want to fulfill their divine mission by helping you ascend.

Let yourself believe in them. Let them be a part of your journey to bring in the new faith currency into your life and into the world.

Many people are still focused on clearing the old blocks. The Unicorns will lift you right out of the old into higher and higher frequencies of Opulence. This will automatically dissolve the old blocks.

The easiest way to start feeling the magical presence of the Unicorns is to receive their blessings.

Your part in this partnership is to receive what they have to offer.

Begin by raising your frequency. Come into the Temple of Pure Gold and let us help you recalibrate in the high vibration of Opulence. As you sit in your calibration chair, breathe, and claim your Oneness with your entire team including the Golden Unicorns.

See the Golden White Unicorns circling in the highest part of this pyramid temple. Watch them continually prance and dance in the celebration of pure Opulence

Open your heart to receive their blessing.

A beautiful Unicorn comes towards you. This Unicorn is an old friend of yours, your personal Unicorn. Embrace its presence and purity.

Let your ancient memories reach back through your many lifetimes and remember your time together.

It may be a subtle feeling, or you may see a scene. Be childlike and use your imagination. What is its name?

Receive your Unicorn's blessing. Open your heart, your mind, your ears, your arms, your entire container, and simply receive.

As you continue to receive the Golden White Unicorns' blessing of Opulence, your personal Unicorn will focus this blessing into your chakras with its horn. See all your chakras lighting up with this Golden Light.

When you are saturated in this blessing, begin to share it everywhere. Send it to your family members, everyone in your life, to places in the world that could use a Unicorn blessing of pure Opulence.

When you go on walks in nature invite your Unicorn to come with you and continue to bless everything that you see. All the nature spirits and elementals will be grateful to receive it.

As you POGO* the Golden Mist into different areas of your life, invite your Unicorn to join your intention and watch the power of the infusion of Opulence increase.

You are not bound by any limitation my friend. Let the gift of this beautiful Unicorn empower your limitless nature.

I AM Manna from Telos

*See Chapter 8, *POGO.*

37

Money Cleansing

There is no more trying to reach us by stretching through the veil. We are with you always. Just call our name or simply say *Golden White Unicorns come* and we immediately respond.

Every time you call on us our relationship will become more real to you. We suggest that you look for evidence of our presence, especially when you are in nature or with animals. As you ask us to send a blessing to an animal, see the response it creates in them.

Today we'd like you to help us cleanse the money, the currency that exists on the planet right now.

Remember money is part of the Elemental Kingdom. The little elementals that are in coins, bills, checks, crypto, in all digital forms of exchange, need our partnership to free them from the burden that humanity has put upon them.

Let's start with the money that is under your care right now.

Take a few minutes to recalibrate yourself in the pyramid Temple of Gold in the 10th sphere with your entire Pure Gold Project team.

Use your sacred inner vision to see or imagine us lovingly radiating Opulence through your physical, mental, emotional, and etheric bodies.

We, the Golden White Unicorns, are circling around the apex of the pyramid, holding the purest frequency of Light. The Angels of Abundance are touching your heart center with the feeling of Opulence. The Masters have their hands outstretched to you sending the Golden Ray of Infinite Abundance, Eternal Peace and the God supply of all that is good to you. The Alpha and Omega Dragons are opening the Light codes within you, helping you to remember your sovereignty, your origin.

You are Opulence.

Drink all of this in with your attention and your breath. Listen to the Music of the Spheres that all this sacred activity is creating and receive.

Now bring all the money in your care and set it on the altar of our Temple.

Talk to your money. Open your heart to it and all the little elementals and electrons that are holding it together. Give it your love. Ask your money to forgive you for all the times you told it that it wasn't enough. Forgive the burden of debt. Forgive yourself for cursing it and not holding it in love.

Call on the Cosmic Diamond Violet Flame to move through you and your money now. See it transmuting all shadow from your money and your relationship to it.

Make a statement of intent on how you will proceed from now on. Make a vow of love to your money and all future money, including the new faith currency.

Now invite us to light up the altar and your money with an infusion of Opulence that will lift your money and the elementals in a permanent Unicorn blessing, filling it with the essence of Pure Gold.

See the altar set ablaze by our horns which create a huge ball of Golden White Light. Join us by holding your hands out in a form of blessing from your heart.

Now Beloved, let's bring all the money in the world onto this altar. It is big enough to hold every means of exchange, large and small.

Together let us raise the frequency of the world's money out of all shadow and darkness into the Light.

We call on Archangels Uriel, Donna Grace, Christiel, and the Angels of Abundance to surround this blessing in the Cosmic Christ Peace so that it is permanently sustained.

It is done.

Thank you for your service. You are a necessary part of this powerful activity of Light. You are the anchors that bring it to the Earth.

Always at your service,

Thom and the Golden White Unicorns

38

Protect your Money

Beloved, a daily decree or prayer becomes a reality. It becomes a physical manifestation in your life.

Have you noticed that as you continue to call in divine protection around yourself and your loved ones daily, that you are shielded from harm in this world?

We encourage you to continue to calibrate daily in the Temple of Pure Gold. The reason is you are building a pathway that is real and tangible. You are paving an avenue for the new faith currency to flow.

We want to encourage you to command God's Invincible Wisdom and Protection over all of your money.

There are many people and companies in the world that are trying to get money from others in illegal and nefarious ways.

When you cloak your money in divine protection and wisdom you will be rising above negative situations.

This is how the new faith currency works. It functions on a higher frequency of Life. It can't be influenced by a dark economy or other people trying to take a ride on your funds.

If you've lost some money in this way, claim it back with your love. Command God's Invincible Wisdom and Protection over the money. Forgive those that scammed you and go through the steps to reclaim it as you would a lost child. See the money coming back to you cleansed and multiplied.

See your money as precious and treat it that way.

The Golden White Unicorns are fierce protectors. Use them this way, Beloved.

As the currencies of the world are changing, bring your questions into the Temple of Pure Gold and we'll help you see the true path to take.

Remember the new faith currency is here to assist all Lightworkers during this time of great transition.

Also, ask the Golden White Unicorns to help you stay in a state of total trust, gratitude, and joy, which will allow miracles to continually happen.

We are with you always.

I love and adore you,

Mother Mary and the Golden White Unicorns

39

Ignite Your Circulation

"The Golden White Unicorns will lift this project, Opulence Infusion, into an entirely new level of manifestation. The Unicorns will make it real. They will bring their magic and transformation in real tangible ways that will open every Lightworker to receive more." ~ Saint Germain

We understand that as a multi-dimensional being living in a human body and in a 3D world can be challenging.

We also want to tell you that to experience the new faith currency now in your physical world, it will require all your faith, some physical action, and some unicorn magic.

The Opulence Infusion can use anything in your world to increase its essence of Pure Gold. Remember the essence of Pure Gold is from the Great Central Sun and is the proof of your total provision and supply in every situation and in any currency. *

Currency means a condition of flowing. **

We want to help you ignite and increase the circulation of money in your life. This is truly a partnership, and this exercise will help you begin to feel us as real and also demonstrate to you the generosity of All That Is.

Every speck of the Beloved Divine is generous. It flows as a giant circle.

Close your eyes and visualize a Golden White Unicorn beside you in a meadow expressing the fullness of springtime.

See your hearts flowing together in perfect harmony.

Ask to be taken into the heart of the Great Central Sun and to 'see' the generosity of the Beloved Divine.

Your Golden White Unicorn invites you to get on its back.

As you begin this journey see the circles of Generosity, as Golden Rays, flowing all around you. Each of them anchored in the Great Central Sun.

Take some time to breathe and receive this vision and this gift of Grace.

As you approach the Great Central Sun your body becomes Pure Light, and ALL becomes One Brilliant Presence. Your inner sight has given way to your open heart as you feel the Truth of who you are in every electron of your being.

Your Unicorn is helping you to receive the full provision and supply, an Opulence Infusion of Generosity, that is your Divine Birthright.

Now allow your Unicorn to seal the light codes of your birthright in every cell of your physical body and all your subtle bodies. Take your time to breathe and receive this wondrous gift.

You feel the movement of your Unicorn bringing you back into your current now, but the Light has not dimmed. It is now a part of you sealed within your physical body.

We are asking you to be generous in your giving. If you want to ignite your circulation of money. Give some away every day in this way.

Give from the generosity of your heart and in appreciation for Life itself. Hold your gift of money up to us, the Golden White Unicorns, or your personal Unicorn, and ask us to bless it with the Opulence Infusion, the new faith currency. See our horns touching your gift with Pure Gold from the Great Central Sun.

In your mind's eye visualize it circulating throughout the world unencumbered. See it circling into the heart of the Great Central Sun and back again.

Now claim it coming right back to you increased and multiplied with the essence of Pure Gold. See it landing right in your wallet, your bank account, in every form of exchange, even unknown forms of currency.

Ask us to continue to flood all your money, your supply, with a Unicorn blessing of generosity.

You can never out-give Source. We challenge you to try it. For this is the gift of generosity.

Enjoy the magic.

Forever yours,

Thom and the Golden White Unicorns.

*The Great Central Sun: God, the owner and giver of ALL LIFE, so far as our galaxy is concerned. It is the sun behind our physical sun and is the source of ALL LIFE and ALL THINGS in the entire galaxy. Werner Schroeder - Lesson 3, "21 Essential Lessons Vol. 1"

**The word currency began in the sixteen hundreds. A "condition of flowing," a sense now rare or obsolete, from Latin currens, present participle of currere "to run" (from PIE root *kers- "to run"). https://www.etymonline.com/word/currency

40

Activate Your Bills

There is no reason for you to wait to begin to use the new faith currency. It is meant to be used now in this time of transition. It can be placed into everything.

We encourage you to make this practical in your everyday experience.

You usually have bills that are on a monthly cycle. This is a good place to show you how to use the Opulence Infusion right now.

Let's bring your Guardian Angel into this activity of Light.

Most of you are under utilizing the divine gift of your personal Angel. They are mighty. Traveling easily between dimensions they can open many doors for you. They have been helping you as you read and experiment with the new faith currency.

Your Angel has trained for centuries in the schools of Light and serves the Beloved Divine by serving you. It is under the direction of your I AM Presence and can only bring your highest good. In other words, you can't direct your Angel to do any harm in any way.

Every time you invite your Angel to participate in whatever you are doing; you are lifted into a greater experience.

Your Angel works in harmony with the Unicorns. We are both members of the Angelic Kingdom.

As your protector and guardian your Angel will open the door to us which allows us to increase your activity a thousand times. We are the purest Light Divine.

Let's activate your bills and debt in the new Opulence Light codes together.

Find a quiet sacred place and focus your attention on your heart. Allow your breath to slow down.

Play Jennifer's song, "Opulence Light Codes," during this activation. *

Visualize all your bills on a floating silver disc right in front of your heart. Notice how you feel about them. Do your best not to judge your own feelings.

Take a few moments to appreciate the services and goods that these bills have brought to you. It could be a warm home, food and clothing, a beauty or health treatment, a new tool for your creativity or business, a new course you wanted to take, or a lesson learned.

Lovingly call on your Guardian Angel to prepare you and your bills to receive the new Opulence Light Codes.

Beloved Guardian Angel, cleanse me and these bills in the Cosmic Diamond Violet Flame. Transmute all negative shadow energy here into the Light of Heaven that never fails. Thank you.

Notice what has happened to the bills on the floating silver disc. See them filled with light and becoming weightless. Be open to any experience that you have.

Now invoke the Golden White Unicorns to crown your bills with the Golden Light of the 10th Sphere.

Beloved Golden White Unicorns activate my bills in the Golden Light of Pure Opulence. Thank you.

We have placed a crown of Golden Light on each of your bills. They now are filled with the new faith currency. Everything you need to pay them is yours.

See them being paid now and those golden crowns carrying the New Opulence Light Codes throughout the world filled with a Golden Unicorn Blessing. They have become a pathway for Ascension.

Do this every time you pay your bills.

You can also do this when you are paying for any service or goods. Simply say, *I crown you with a Golden White Unicorn Blessing of Opulence.*

This is a great service to yourself, your household, and to the entire planet.

Take a moment to give thanks for this gift you've received and distributed today.

Forever Yours,

Thom and the Golden White Unicorns

*"Opulence Light Codes" is on Jennifer's *Opulence EP*.

41

Storehouses of Gold

We want to focus your attention today on the storehouses of Pure Gold that are here for you in every dimension of this Universe. It will help you bypass the old systems that are being dismantled.

I AM the God of Gold and I bring with me today the Lords of Gold, the Angels of Gold, and the Golden White Unicorns. We are the caretakers and the guardians of the storehouses of Infinite Supply, Pure Gold.

Take a few minutes to breath the essence of Pure Gold into your Auric Field.

Breathe it in the shape of a Golden Infinity sign that passes through your heart. See this Infinity sign growing and growing as it reaches deep into the Earth and high into the Cosmos with each breath. Take your time.

Invoke us to increase this transmission beyond your own understanding.

Surrender to the pure innocence and brilliance of this radiation. Allow yourself to receive and be infused with this Golden essence.

Begin to move the Golden Infinity sign slowly to the right with each breath.

At the peak of each inhale and the release of each exhale, take a short pause. During that pause you are connecting with a storehouse of Pure Opulence at different supply centers throughout the cosmos, on and within the Earth.

Now still your breath and come into complete stillness. You are a lightning rod of Opulence loaded and ready.

With your focused attention now direct it into anything that needs supply and beauty. Start with yourself and your household. Then continue to expand it throughout your neighborhood, your territory, and then into the world.

If you feel you need more, come back to your Golden Infinity breath, and reload.

The storehouses of Pure Gold will never be depleted. In fact, when you use the storehouses this way, they increase the supply. It will never run out, Beloved. It will never run out for you, no matter what circumstances you are in.

Close your eyes and see the Golden White Unicorns circling around you now, sealing this experience so you can continue to build on it.

This supply of Pure Gold is your standard. Let go of the old measuring system of big is better. Let go of the old process of measuring yourself against a number or someone else's idea of success.

Bypass the old system by using the multidimensional storehouses of this Universe.

We are with you always,

God of Gold, Lords of Gold, Angels of Gold, and the Golden White Unicorns

42

Numbers and Dollars

Beloveds, it is time to dismantle the hold that numbers (including how many likes on social media) and dollar amounts keep you tethered to the old.

We want to make it clear that as long as you are holding on to the old system, it will keep controlling you, making you feel like a victim, and keep you in fear.

As you become more confident in the new faith currency, you'll begin to see this old structure of fear and manipulation fall from your shoulders and release in your belly, especially within your solar plexus.

Ask for our assistance in helping you. It's your choice how quickly you want to step into the new faith currency and be a part of the new Opulence Infusion.

As you know, it's much easier to complain than it is to make a decision and insist on its fulfillment.

Don't let what you see in your bank account make your decision for you. Don't let it define your divine inheritance of Pure Opulence.

We suggest that you move your focus from your bank account to the Storehouses of Pure Gold that are available to you. (See Chapter 41)

Withdraw emotionally and mentally from social media and the game of likes and agreement. It is a false game.

If you enter this forum with the desire to be validated, accepted, and liked, you are stepping into a den of hungry lions.

You get to decide what social media will be for you. It will offer you what you want it to.

It's the same wherever you measure success by numbers and dollars. Especially in bringing your gifts and offerings to the world.

As with everything about you and your life, you are the one that must make the choice.

Saint Germain said it so well, "You are the only energizer of your world and all it contains. When you think or feel, part of your life energy goes forth to sustain your creation." *

Everything moves in a natural divine flow.

Allow yourself to move out of the old heaviness of numbers and dollars and come with us into the Glory of the Opulence Infusion, a new faith currency.

The time is now.

We are with you always.

We love and adore you,

Mother Mary, the Angels of Abundance, Thom, and the Golden White Unicorns

P.S. Make keeping track of your finances a spiritual practice of joy.

*"*Unveiled Mysteries*" – Saint Germain

43

You are the Bridge

I AM your personal Unicorn.

Come with me. Today I'd like to take you for a ride.

I see the purity of your heart. I see you as Love Itself. I'm grateful to be by your side on this journey of Ascension.

Come and get up on my back. I want to show you your place in this groundbreaking spiritual technology we are calling a new faith currency, an Opulence infusion.

We are climbing up into the upper atmosphere of Mother Earth and circling the globe.

See the land masses and the water and connect with Mother Gaia, the Devas, and the Nature Spirits that are working on the eco system to sustain the divine flow.

Notice the places that are pure and untouched by mankind. See the harmony of the eternal song being sung by all life, including the people that live there.

Now notice the places that are struggling to maintain life. The war zones, the scarring from overusing the natural resources and the cities that are overpopulated. Notice the disharmony of people suffering in lack, feeling unsafe, and scrambling to get their basic human needs met.

Hold on, we are going to dive through the surface of the earth and into hollow inner earth. You are completely protected and safe on this journey.

Feel that sense of leaving time as you move into a feeling of suspended peace. Notice the beauty of the Diamond Light everywhere. Listen to the songs of life in harmony.

See the crystals and mineral kingdoms, including the strands of silver and gold, glistening, and shining the Light of Heaven throughout the surfaces. Nature is showing off exquisite trees and flowers that you've never seen before.

The sky, the water, the mountains and valleys, the neighborhoods, and cities, take your breath away.

The Agartha network of Inner Earth has set up civilizations of peace and divine government. They live in the higher dimensions of Oneness. You can see people's full auras filled with the Rainbow Rays. They are shining in true spiritual freedom.

There are many Unicorns, Dragons, and Angels that work here. All the animals live in harmony with each other, the plants, and the residents.

We are now going into the Cave of Creation flying over the millions of crystals that are held here for all of mankind on the surface.

I'm pointing my horn of gold to your crystal.

Your heart immediately opens in joy as you recognize it. Slip off my back and touch your crystal. Stand on it. Instantly feel the eternal purpose of your life from the fullness of your I AM Presence, your Monad, ignite every part of your being.

Feel the connection from your crystal to the Great Central Sun. The Great Central Sun Magnet is drawing you back HOME.

See a strong beam of Golden Christ Light moving up and down in a continuous motion right through you, lighting up your chakras.

Stay here for a few minutes and breath this experience into your subtle bodies, allowing yourself the time to fully receive it.

Feel into the many lifetimes on the surface that have prepared you to be a catalyst at this time. To bring in the new faith currency through the illusion that you've experienced of lack, deprivation, scarcity, and separation.

See yourself as the magnet that is drawing the Opulence Infusion throughout the entire surface of the planet.

Thank your crystal in the Cave of Creation for anchoring you and your divine mission.

Now come onto my back once again and we're going to ride up your beam of Golden Christ Light together.

As we reach the surface of the Earth, notice the circle of Golden White Dragons that have joined us, circling us, and increasing the beam of Light as we rise.

Command your beam of Light to flood the Earth and energize it with Pure Opulence, Pure Gold. See it filling every nook and cranny of life.

Notice what is happening to the planet.

What do you see?

What has happened to those places that have been devastated due to war and famine?

What do the cities look like now?

Focus on some of the people that had been suffering in limitation, what has happened to them?

Give thanks for your journey and your victory.

We have safely landed back in your current now.

Thank you for coming with me today. You are the connector, a bridge, to pull in the new faith currency. You are a mighty force.

You are the Pure Light of the Beloved Divine. We couldn't do this without you.

I love you,

Your Personal Unicorn and the Golden White Unicorns

44

I AM a Living Transmission of Opulence

Remember the Golden White Unicorns will ignite and increase every step you take in your ascension as a living transmission of Opulence.

The choice is yours, Beloved. Will you choose to be a living transmission of Opulence and flow the new faith currency through your daily life?

If your answer is 'Yes', we want to seal your choice permanently not only within you, but also in our eternal partnership. This will establish it in the Earth as a real and tangible supply in service to all.

To begin, face the east and stand in a powerful stance.

Call on your Mighty, I AM Presence, your Monad and feel your 12 - 5th dimensional chakras opening the 12 x 12 aspects of your being in the Golden Mist.

Speak out loud 3 times:

I AM the Monad. I AM the Light Divine. I AM Love. I AM Wisdom. I AM Will. I AM Fixed Design.

Speak your commitment out loud 3 times.

I will to be a Living Transmission of Opulence now and forever.

As you stand in your power bring your attention to your team in the Pure Gold Project Pyramid Lab in the 10th Sphere of Infinite Abundance, Eternal Peace and the God Supply of every good thing. (Chapter 1)

Raise your hands up to receive our full transmission of Opulence. Allow us to bring to you a living activation of the Golden Pyramid.

See the Pyramid fully intact being lowered all around you.

Breathe.

See the base of the Golden Pyramid grounded into your Earth Star Chakra. The entire Pyramid is flooding Opulence through all your Chakras and rising to completely fill your Lightbody, your Mighty I AM Presence, your Monad.

We are right here with you. We have permanently sealed your choice and our partnership on every dimension.

Let this be your mantra. "I AM a Living Transmission of Opulence now and forever."

We love and adore you,

Mother Mary, the Golden White Unicorns, the Angels of Abundance, and your entire Pure Gold Team

45

Commanding Presence

Beloved, you are a Commanding Presence.

We have moved through igniting your circulation, receiving the blessings of the Golden White Unicorns, lifting your money, protecting your money, crowning your bills, being a living transmission of Opulence ... everything will be amplified as you step into your Commanding Presence.

Ask yourself, "What do I want?"

Ask yourself this question several times to get under the surface to the real desire. *

To be effective in your commanding, follow these simple steps. They will help you be aligned with your true power and not from your powerless feeling of being a victim.

In the morning, move through your daily spiritual practice of connecting, aligning, and protecting.

Come into your heart and join with your Beloved I AM Presence. Surrender your little human ego to the Magnificence of your Monad, your Eternal Self.

Ask Archangel Michael to place his Powerful cloak of Protection around you.

Connect with your Pure Gold Project team, including the Golden White Unicorns, and recalibrate to the frequency of Pure Opulence, the new faith currency.

Now you are ready. You are in alignment with your true nature. You are a commanding Presence.

Step into your Divine Authority and speak this decree 3 times:

I Am the Commanding Presence, the Exhaustless Energy, the Divine Wisdom, and Love causing the manifestation of _____ (your desire) to be fulfilled, now. **

Take this decree with you throughout the day and repeat it whenever you can. You are building the strength of your desire and taking your right place in service to the Most High.

Every time you step into the Commanding Presence of your Mighty I AM, your Unicorn, the Angels and the Elementals and your entire team immediately come to attention and expand your command.

Accept who you are Beloved. You are powerful and precious.

I love and adore you,

Mother Mary and the Golden White Unicorns

*We hear many people say that they want more money. Keep going to the deeper desire. What would the money be used for? What would it bring you? What does it have to do with your ascension?

If you are ignoring a life lesson that has been knocking on your door, pay attention to what you have asked to learn here. Commanding that the lesson leave, is not the answer for you. That's why taking the time to go beneath the outer is important.

If you are stuck in an initiation and feel that you are in a blind spot, see a Practitioner of Truth that has a relationship with the Beloved Divine, and ask for some assistance.

** Decree adapted from *I AM Discourses, Vol 3*

46

Multiply

Beloved, I, Saint Germain, want to remind you today of an ancient law that you can use right now. It is part of the new faith currency that uses spiritual alchemy to increase what is already physically present.

The definition of the word multiply is to increase or cause to increase greatly in number or quantity.

Remember the story of Hanukkah. The temple was to be destroyed. And the faithful community knew that if they could keep the oil lamp burning it would be saved. There was only oil enough for one day but through prayer it was increased for eight days. This is a story of faith, freedom, and the use of the Law of Multiplication.

In the Old Testament there is a story of Elijah in 1 Kings 17:8-24. He was told there was a widow in Sidon that would take care of him while he was there. When they met, the widow was gathering wood to prepare the last meal for herself and her son before they died of starvation. All she had was a handful of flour in a jug and little bit of oil in a jar. Elijah told her to prepare the bread, to eat it with her son, and then bring some to him. He promised her that the jug of flour and the jar of oil would never be empty. And it never was.

Elijah was an embodiment of Metatron. He was a powerful prophet and had an important divine mission.

Your divine mission is just as important, my friend. These stories were built into your DNA and the memories of your cells. However, they are not to remain there. They are to be used now as part of the new faith currency.

Through your DIVINE AUTHORITY, your Beloved I AM Presence, and the 3-fold Flame of your heart, you can command what you require to live and to complete your divine mission in ease.

Use this divine alchemy in your everyday life and expect the miracle.

Do you need to increase the gas in your fuel tank? Do you need to increase the dollars within your bank account or food in your pantry?

Begin by disengaging from the old ideas of supply and demand. You run out of something, and you go out to get it from a source in the world.

Start experimenting with the Law of Multiplication and soon you'll be perfecting your skills.

As the world continues to change rapidly including the usual supply chains, you'll be using these skills more and more.

Don't be discouraged if you don't see results right away. Practice every day until you see the manifestation, Beloved.

Remember I am a Master of Divine Alchemy. Invite me and the Golden White Unicorns to help you start to practice multiplying what you already have.

Go to the place where you want to see the increase such as your car, your wallet, your bank statement, etc.

Stand in your Divine Authority and concentrate. Focus your energy.

Speak this out loud three times:

I set into action my Beloved I AM Presence, Beloved Saint Germain, and the Law of Multiplication. I command an infusion of Opulence to multiply and increase _____ (name what it is) now. Beloved Golden White Unicorns (or your personal Unicorn) place your Golden horn(s) here and assist to increase this supply now. Thank you.

Begin to see yourself as a Divine Alchemist for this is who you are.

Always at your service,

Saint Germain and the Golden White Unicorns

47

The Flame of Adoration

Begin this chapter from a calm meditative state, fully protected in the Light.

Let's go for a journey. Lift up onto the back of your Golden White Unicorn and let us take you on a journey. We want to show you something from our perspective. We think it will help you in multiplying the pure gold essence.

As we rise into the 10th sphere, one dimension at a time. Feel the weight of the old system falling away from you. See it shedding as a snake's skin from your auric field.

This heavy burden has been with you for so long that it feels like it's a part of you. It is not. It is the old cloak of fear that has been instilled in you around money and supply for thousands of years.

This fear has created an imbalance in your creative triangle, the 3-fold flame of your heart. As we move through the City of Gold, breathe in the Golden Mist, and let it fill your heart.

Let it flood through the will of your Blue Flame.

See the Golden Mist expanding your mind with Illumined Wisdom of the Sunshine Yellow Flame.

Now feel it saturating the Unconditional Love of the Crystalline Pink Flame in your heart.

As we come into the Pure Gold Lab, feel the welcoming embrace of your Beloved Team and take a seat in your calibration chair. Continue to breathe into your 3-fold flame as you listen to one of Jennifer's songs of Opulence and recalibrate.

Please take your time.

Remember what you are currently multiplying and see it in front of you.

We notice that many of you are using your will and your intelligence to create. This is only part of the equation of your co-creation. If your love isn't in balance with the other two you will be pushing, pulling, and striving instead of receiving.

Your love is the power. It is the most important part of being a living transmission of Opulence and building the new faith currency.

Now bring that which you are multiplying once again into your awareness.

Invoke Archangel Chamuel and your Beloved Unicorn to assist you.

Through the authority of my 3-fold Flame I call Beloved Chamuel, the Archangel of Adoration, and my Golden White Unicorn to flood the Sacred Fire of Adoration, the Crystalline Pink Ray, into _____ (what you are multiplying).

See your creation surrounded in this Pink Light.

See your Golden White Unicorn touch it with its horn and expand it from the inside out.

This Mighty Pink Ray is the Law of Multiplication.

Now bring the strength of the Blue Ray in and through your creation as it joins the Pink Ray.

Finally bring in the Illumined Wisdom that contains the perfect idea and perception of Pure Opulence to complete this triad of creation.

We encourage you to always begin with the Crystalline Pink Ray of Adoration as you use the Law of Multiplication.

This Ray will bring you out of the heavy burden of the old and put you on a new level of creating.

See your creation sealed in the 3-fold flame and release it to the Law of Creation and Multiplication.

Take a ride of freedom and joy with your Golden White Unicorn as you come back into your current now.

We are thrilled to be building the new faith currency on Earth with you.

In Joyful Expectation,

Thom, Archangel Chamuel, and the Golden White Unicorns.

48

Riding the Waves

I have brought you to this Pure Gold Project because you are a change agent. You are the ones that are bringing financial freedom in the form of a new faith currency, an Opulence infusion, to the Earth currently.

It is my great honor to lead you forward. I AM the commander and chief of this Age of Freedom and Justice. We also call it the Age of Miracles. I AM Saint Germain.

You are stepping out of the Information Age and into Divine Energy. The currents of the Mighty Rays move you out of your thinking mind of how things work. What you have stored in your brain or saved on your computer is old news.

Now it's time to ride on the Divine Waves of Light.

As conductors of Divine Energy, your partnership with us; the Ascended Ones, the Angelic Realm, which includes the Unicorns, the Elemental Kingdom, and the Dragon Brigade, is empowering you to move quickly on these Waves of Light into your ascension.

Financial freedom used to mean that you had accumulated a lot of money. This perspective on security asks the question, "How much are you worth?" As if an amount of money could tell you what you are worth.

You can bypass this entire system of accumulated wealth and flow the new faith currency, the essence of Pure Gold, where it is required.

This flow will help you immensely if you've decided you are on a fixed income or when the economy goes up and down or crashes. It is also helpful when you need something that doesn't appear to be available in your physical world.

There's only one Truth, you are the Opulence of the Beloved Divine. This Truth will never change. It is always and forever the only absolute Truth.

There is a difference between knowing and living this Truth.

You are a living transmission of Opulence. Your job, if you choose to accept it, is to move and conduct this energy. It is ALIVE and PURE. Your command sets it into action in your life and in the world around you.

Your ego mind will always try to get you to go backwards into what you know from the past.

Beloved, the past is dissolving, and you are now fully entering into a new system of manifestation.

Let go and move forward.

To use these Mighty Waves of Light, also known as the Sacred Rays, you become them and command them into action.

Just as you turn on a switch to light up a room. You can use this Divine Energy immediately.

As your Heavenly Team, we amplify and multiply your command. Every time you speak our names, we are immediately present.

You are the one, Beloved that gets to choose. Follow the desires of your heart.

Your I AM Presence is your command center.

Your team on the ground includes your guardian angel, and your ancestral guides, your personal unicorn, your personal dragon, your body elemental, and your team of elementals. All of them are directed by your Holy Christ/Buddha Self.

They will help you stay in a state of trust, purity, and miracle readiness.

I urge you to experiment with conducting the Golden Ray of Infinite Abundance, Eternal Peace, and God's supply of every good thing. Practice is daily.

You are building your spiritual strength. Think of yourself as a Jedi. Get out your light saber and conduct Opulence as you ride the Divine Waves of Light.

I'm grateful to be leading you onward. I'm thankful for your presence, Beloved and your service to bring a new kind of financial freedom into the Aquarian Age.

You are always in my heart,

Saint Germain and the Pure Gold Project team

49

Heal Your Inner Critic

Beloved, as a living transmission of Opulence your life will change. You will be expanding as a glowing light and others will be drawn to you and your energy. You will become more visible to those that are ready to hear the message of the new faith currency.

Becoming more visible is a gift. It is another great opportunity for you to release the old ideas that you are not enough and you're not doing it right.

Within the Lightworkers community we hear the call for the dissolution of the inner critic. We see this gray cloud of disapproval and self-judgment. It's a toxic energy that's hanging in the auric fields of all mankind.

Healing this voice is part of your ascension journey.

It is time for the transmutation of this old way of being with yourself. Your chance to break this cycle is now.

Although the inner voice probably sounds like the voice of one of your parents or guardians, we are asking you to see it as a voice that is part of the collective human experience.

Notice where this voice rises and becomes louder. It is doing its best to suppress your growth as a spiritual leader and a living transmission of Opulence.

Take the time with us today to begin taking dominion over your inner critic.

Command your freedom Beloved, for the inner critic is no longer serving you in any way. It is part of the ego mind that wants to remain in control. Underneath that control is a call for Love.

Begin by making a declaration. Stand in front of a mirror, look into your own eyes, and begin tapping on your body, and say out loud:

Inner critic, although I have listened to you for a long time, I am no longer interested in what you have to say. You are not part of my true self. You have no power over me. Through the divine authority of my Beloved I AM Presence I command you, in love, to step down now. I AM Love and Love is the only voice that I choose to hear.

Call on your Guardian Angel, your Body Elemental, the Angels of Abundance, your personal fire Dragon, and your Unicorn. Ask them to support your declaration and to transmute and etherealize this ancient voice, in every electron of your auric field, into a voice of only Love.

Place a picture of yourself that you especially like on your altar. See yourself walking into the world as a spiritual leader, following your calling in poise and confidence as you become more and more visible.

Notice when your inner critic starts to activate. Blaze the Violet Flame over your picture and speak your declaration again followed by the Ho'oponopono prayer.

"I love you. I'm sorry. Please forgive me. Thank you."

You will start to feel the melting of this voice as it receives your love and forgiveness.

Stay with this process until the inner critic etherealizes into Love.

We are assisting you every step of the way as you move through the 4th dimension into your spiritual freedom and leadership.

I love and adore you,

Mother Mary, the Angels of Abundance, and Thom

Singing the *Ho'oponopono Prayer Chant* in Jennifer's music collection is very helpful.

50

Choose Again and Again

Beloved, our third eye power naturally developed our golden horns. The power of our hearts in deep love for the All That Is, built this focus from our pure desire.

Many times, in your dimension when a desire is birthed, it is from an experience of lack.

It brings your focus into a pure desire of something you'd like to change in your life or in the world.

It may make you angry and frustrated, and that energy is powerful.

These intense feelings will help you begin to feel and see your pure desire. Receive this awakening into what needs to be changed.

Own your desire instead of pushing it away and surrender it to your Beloved I AM Presence.

This practice gives the divine blueprint of your desire a chance to gestate from within.

As you begin to nurture this desire with your attention, call us in to help you birth it into manifestation.

We can help you stay focused. For in this phase of creation, we see many of you losing the intensity that your desire first stirred in you.

As you start to experience the new faith currency here and there in your everyday life, the pure desire for it seems to lessen a bit and you can get sloppy with your part of co-creation.

Stay with the third eye focus. It will have a different energy. Not the intensity of anger, but a daily practice of intention.

As the creator of this desire, you are required to nurture it. Don't give up before the manifestation.

The only thing that is stunting the growth of your desire is your daily focus.

Stand by your desire and let us help you increase the intensity of your third eye power.

Your pure desire will heal anything within you that is keeping it away from you.

Get a complete picture in your mind of what the fulfillment of this desire would look like.

Place it in the crystal lens of your third eye and spend time every day holding it there.

Call on Archangel Raphael, your personal Unicorn, and the Golden White Unicorns of the 10th Golden Ray, to help strengthen and expand your efforts.

Write a short powerful decree from the complete picture of your pure desire and repeat it often.

You can tailor the decree below to fit your own desire.

I AM experiencing a beautiful new home that fits my life perfectly, beyond what I can even imagine. I command all logistics, details, and funds that are required to be made visible now. In the name of my Beloved Presence, I AM, I release this desire to the Giver of all Life.

Choose your pure desire daily. Choose it again and again and again. *

Allow the waves of Opulence to infuse your desire.

Invite us to assist you every step of the way. Giving you assistance fulfills the divine mission of our current presence here.

In Pure Delight,

THOM and the Golden White Unicorns

*Pure Desire: Feel me, see me, awaken to me, and claim me as your own. Birth me, then nurture me, stand by me, and choose me. Choose again and again and again.

From the song, "No Fear," from Jennifer Ruth Russell's CD *Worthy*

51

Your Sweet Spot

There is a sweet balance between choosing and surrender. This sweet spot is a state of miracle readiness.

As you choose and then surrender you are in the arena of creation.

If you choose without letting your team join you in bringing about the manifestation, you are missing out on the joy of our partnership. You are also missing out on the union of our hearts that takes you beyond the limitation of human thought.

If you just surrender without choice, you are not honoring your own divine purpose here on Earth. You're not participating in the free will that you've been given. You are not using your personal power.

You came here to remember your powerful presence as a conductor of divine energy.

The best choices come from your communion with your Beloved I Am Presence. A good choice will always give you a juicy feeling of the Love of Life.

When you choose to let your Beloved I AM Presence help with your choices, it is your ticket to quickening your joyful ascension. This is a beautiful surrendering of co-creation at the highest level.

Beloved, I encourage you to find this sweet spot every morning before you go about your day. You may feel it in your heart, your third eye, or your solar plexus ... or all three.

Visualize your desire completely fulfilled. See it already manifested. Give it back to your Beloved I AM Presence.

Ask your Beloved Unicorn to radiate the high rarified purity of its octave into your sweet spot.

Now ask the rest of your Pure Gold team to help you maintain your choice and surrender throughout the day.

Beloved, enjoy this privilege to choose. It creates miracles.

We love and adore you,

Mother Mary, THOM, and the entire Pure Gold Project Team

52

Circle of Cleansing Light

Beloved, we want to lead you through a cleansing of all human thought and concern today.

Your auric field requires daily cleansing. The subtleties of your thoughts that aren't spoken or even noticed can impede your progress.

We'll remind you again and again to use us. We will accelerate your ascension and your use of the new faith currency.

Take some time to center in your Beloved I AM Presence.

Ask Archangel Michael to surround you in his protection shield of royal blue.

Ground into your Earth Star Chakra.

Call in your personal dragon to carry you into the 10th Sphere of Infinite Abundance, Eternal Peace, and the God supply of all that is good.

As you stroll with your dragon through the City of Gold, breathe in the Golden Mist and relax in the Opulence.

Come into the Pyramid Temple of Pure Gold and feel the embrace of your heavenly team.

Come and sit in your calibration chamber and listen to one of Jennifer's light songs to prepare you.

Let your breath be your focus.

Sense the Golden Dragons forming a circle around you. Welcome them.

The Angels of Abundance join them in a higher wider circle. Acknowledge their presence.

Now tune into our presence, the Golden White Unicorns, in a circle high above you. Let your heart open and embrace us.

We our placing our horns in the center of this circle of Opulence. We are radiating Pure White and Gold Light into this Circle of Light.

From your seat we are asking you to place your concerns, worries, fears, burdens, and prayers within this circle one at a time through your mind. Stay in silence.

Use your in-breath to identify the prayer and with your out-breath place it in the circle of cleansing Light and let it go.

Begin with yourself and your subtle bodies; your physical, etheric, mental, and emotional, bodies.

Keep going with any concerns about your health, your bills, your dreams, your family, any detail of your life.

Now place your loved ones in this cleansing circle.

Be thorough. We want to assist you in completely letting go of all burdens and placing it all in Father Mother's tender loving care.

Keep expanding out through your neighborhood, your city, your territory, your country, and the world.

Focus your breath now on the hot spots around the globe.

When you feel complete. Speak out loud, *I completely let go and let Spirit bring the highest solution to everything that I've placed here. I give thanks, it is done. I AM FREE. And so it is!*

Now visualize the Golden Dragons, the Angels of Abundance, and all the Golden White Unicorns moving this circle upward as answered prayer. It is done.

Your beloved personal Dragon is ready to take you back to your current now.

Give thanks for this release.

Come back often to the Cleansing Circle of Light to refresh.

We are yours,

THOM

The Golden White Unicorns

The Angels of Abundance

The Golden Dragons

53

Faith Expansion

Sometimes you may feel that nothing is happening or changing. This is not true. The calls that you are making, the insistence of being a living transmission of Opulence, the visualizations, and exercises that we've taken you thorough in this book are moving the old stagnant energy of lack, limitation, scarcity, fear, and depravity in every cell, atom, and electron of your entire being.

We have called this a faith currency because it always begins and ends with your faith.

The beautiful thing about faith is that it easily grows by your attention to it. Moving your thoughts to a state of trust will always bring a universal response to you and begin to provide immediately.

You can't choose fear and faith at the same time. You are asked to clearly choose one or the other.

If you feel yourself caught in a pocket of fear and it feels like it is taking you down a black hole of despair, use your choice to choose again.

Remember fear is of the little mind and has no power over you unless you choose it.

Use your grit and your will to make the demand. You are commanding every spec of Divine Energy within you to move.

Call on us and we'll lead you out of the forest. Your faith is also required to believe in us. All you need is a little bit of faith, which you already have, and we'll increase it.

Stop whatever you are doing, sit in a quiet place and light a candle. This signifies a ritual is starting and alerts all the Angels, including us, to pay attention.

Close your eyes and begin to breathe slowly. Watch your breath and feel your body calm down and center.

See your breath as your faith and breathe in a deep royal blue color. This color is of the 1st Ray of Divine Will, Faith, Trust, Courage, and Surrender.

Stay out of your mind as much as you can. Now visualize each of your 12 chakras, like a string of blue pearls, filling up with the magnificent royal blue.

Call on your personal unicorn and the Golden White Unicorns from the pyramid Temple of Pure Gold to radiate their high rarified purity through each of your chakras.

See your chakras releasing all fear as the 1st Ray takes over.

Ask us to help you increase the strength and substance of your faith.

Don't rush. This process is well worth your time for we are helping you grow the muscle of your faith.

Stay with us in this faith ritual until you feel the deep calm of the Christ Buddha Peace settle in your solar plexus.

Finally ask Archangel Michael to seal your faith permanently in his Prevention Flame. Keep the momentum of your faith growing and invincibly protected.

Forever yours,

Thom and the Golden White Dragons

54

Pure Heart

I hold the purity of your heart, Beloved.

As you come into the union of our hearts, you lift into the purity of my heart. We are one.

I Am the best of you. I Am you.

Our union gives you full access to my high vibration of purity. Use it.

By grafting your heart to mine it gives you the ability to hear the crystal-clear voice of your Beloved. Our voice opens your inner ear and becomes one beautiful gift of direction and guidance for you.

Abundance flows through the purity of our heart union.

During this time of great change our union becomes even more significant and important for you.

Staying in a state of purity will help you navigate through mass panic and confusion. It will allow you to make the highest choices and move swiftly out of harm's way.

Our heart connection is a Sanctuary for you, physically, mentally, and spiritually.

Surround and purify your money in the Beloved Divine's wisdom and protection.

Remember to take the time daily to come into the stillness and receive guidance.

The Opulence Infusion you are receiving requires your participation to help distribute it in your life, which continually establishes it on Earth.

Pay attention to the signs along the way. They are everywhere for you. You are here to participate in building the Divine Earth.

As you continue to come into the union of our hearts everything you need to know will be revealed to you, as you need to know it.

The stillness of our union is your lifeline.

I Am the best of you. I Am you.

I love and adore you,

Mother Mary and the Angels of Abundance

55

Command the Age of Miracles

Beloved, what a delight it has been to be with you through the pages of this book and in all dimensions of the Light that never fails.

Keep on with your daily applications of being a living transmission of Opulence.

Remember you are the ground team for the distribution of the new faith currency. It is living and breathing through and as your life. You are a conscious conductor of Pure Gold.

You will always be able to ride the waves above the chaos and confusion of change.

Embrace the unknown. See the many changes that are taking place as the fulfillment of the Divine Plan.

Our union will continue to be the mighty force in your life. Remember this is a conduit of the Opulence Infusion.

Abundance flows through my Immaculate Heart. I Am a Unicorn Master. I Am a Universal Archangel. I Am your friend in very high places.

I love to assist you in demonstrating your own power as you conduct the new faith currency where it is required.

Where are we going from here?

Command that this Age of Miracles be your everyday life. Command money miracles (in all forms) to be your continuous experience.

We are with you always.

We love and adore you,

Mother Mary, and the entire Pure Gold Project Team

Dedication

I dedicate this book to anyone on a mystical journey who is ready to embrace your creative power and ascension and to those of you who love Spirit so much that the call of your heart is greater than anything in this world.

My beloved family of Light may you no longer suffer in self-doubt and limitation.

May you step into your power as a wealthy Light Engineer in this unprecedented time of rapid reconstruction of the Divine New Earth.

We need you now more than ever before.

I created the Angels of Abundance Ascension Academy and Creative Abundance with Mother Mary because I am passionate about empowering Light beings to become strong financially as we ascend. It is an important initiation for each one of us.

Mother Mary and I'd love to continue this journey with you.

In Love and Joyful Abundance,

Jennifer

AngelsofAbundanceAscensionAcademy.com

You can find all of Jennifer's recordings here:
https://jenniferruthrussell.bandcamp.com/music/

Acknowledgements

I give thanks for the gentle insistence of Saint Germain, Mother Mary, the Angels of Abundance, and the entire Pure Gold Project Team to download these powerful messages that are helping us change from victimhood into victorious creators. The new faith currency is a game changer.

I am grateful for the precious Family of Light of the Angels of Abundance Ascension Academy for calling this book forward and for completing the circle of this inquiry.

I give thanks for all the teachers that have gone before me and influenced my journey of true Wealth and Abundance: Jeshua, Saint Germain, Archangel Michael, Metatron, Godfrey King, Ronna Herman, Auriela Louise Jones, Patricia Cota-Robles, Caroline Oceana Ryan, the Sophia Dragon Tribe Mentors and Kaia Ra, the I AM Discourses, the Bridge to Freedom work, Catherine Ponder, Ernest Holmes, Eric Butterworth, John Randolph Price, Elizabeth Clare Prophet, Edwine Gaines, Michael Bernard Beckwith, Rev. Margaret Shepherd, Rev. Karen Russo, and Jessica Hadari.

I give thanks to my beloved prayer partners Taffy Wallace and Andrea Lane who continually remind me of who I am.

I give thanks to Michelle Walker for her joyful creation of *Opulence* that adorns the front cover of this book and her friendship. I give thanks for the Awesome out-of-the-box Goddess mastermind group that always calls me to think higher.

Special thanks to Julaina Kleist for lovingly keeping me within the lines by editing this little book and Elizabeth MacFarland, my graphic designer, who always brings a sparkle of excellence to everything.

I am grateful for my son Andy and my entire family who continues to show me what unconditional love is.

I am extremely grateful for my beloved husband and partner, Michael Gayle, who always supports everything I do, produces all my music, and brings sunshine into my life every day.

About the Author

Jennifer has been a Spiritual Mentor for more than 20 years. She trained at Agape International Spiritual Center, in Culver City, California, under Rev. Michael Bernard Beckwith. She has mentored thousands of clients and students in the depths of financial lack and heartache, helping them to heal their hearts and lives by connecting to the Light of their own Divinity.

Jennifer is the creator of Angels of Abundance Ascension Academy and Creative Abundance with Mother Mary. As your money blueprint is transformed you become a living transmission of Opulence. When you are deeply nurtured and nudged to step into your sovereignty and divine authority, you flourish.

Her intimate partnership with Mother Mary, Archangel Michael, Saint Germain and the entire Company of Heaven is the unseen force that runs her ministry.

Jennifer is also an award-winning songwriter. Songs have always poured out of her heart. She loves to take people into the stillness of the soul and the playfulness of the light. She has written and recorded thirteen CDs, including her award-winning *Virtues Songs A-Z* for children.

Jennifer's life vision is to uplift and empower Lightworkers to live abundantly and transform the world with songs and prayers that open the heart. When you are in her presence you will feel the deep connection of the Angels.

A moment with Jennifer is like immersing yourself in the inspiration of the best music and the love of a most powerful prayer. – Rev. Michael Bernard Beckwith

Jennifer Russell channels the warmth and loving energies of Mother Mary, offering the higher frequency of that beautiful Ascended Being's compassion and understanding of our human complexities where money and Abundance are concerned. – Caroline Oceana Ryan

Music opens our hearts in ways that nothing else can. When Jennifer Russell shares her beautiful music and sings her heartfelt songs, there is an undeniable stirring in every heart and an Awakening that seems to move us forward in the Light in new and profound ways. - Patricia Cota-Robles

Printed in Great Britain
by Amazon